PRAISE FOR CLA[...] P9-ELI-037

'A knockout new talent you should read immediately.'

—Lee Child

'It really had me gripped.'
    —Marian Keyes, international bestselling author of *Grown Ups*

'The definition of an utterly absorbing page turner. Richly drawn out characters, a compelling plot, and a finale that will keep you guessing.'
    —John Marrs, bestselling author of *What Lies Between Us* and
The One

'A real nailbiter of a thriller that gets darker and more twisted with every page. If you liked *What You Did*, you'll love *The Push*.'
—Erin Kelly, *Sunday Times* bestselling author of *He Said/She Said*

'Absorbing, timely, and beautifully written, *What You Did* is a superior psychological thriller from a major talent.'
    —Mark Edwards, bestselling author of *The Retreat* and
Here to Stay

'I loved this story. The flesh-and-blood characters, dry wit, and brilliant plotting are every bit as enjoyable as *Big Little Lies*.'
    —Louise Candlish, bestselling author of *Our House* and
The Other Passenger

'A perfectly-plotted murder mystery had me hooked from the first page. Twisty domestic suspense that's perfect for fans of *Big Little Lies*.'
    —Lisa Gray, bestselling author of the Jessica Shaw series

'I haven't flown through a book so quickly in a very long time. It delivers on every single level.'
—Caz Frear, bestselling author of the DC Cat Kinsella series

'What a nail-biting, just-one-more-page-I-can't-put-it-down rollercoaster of suspense!'
—Steph Broadribb, author of *Deep Down Dead*

'Smart, sassy, and satisfyingly twisty.'
—Sarah Hilary, author of the DI Marnie Rome series

'Huge fun with some very dark moments and brilliantly awful characters. Excellent, twisty plotting.'
—Harriet Tyce, author of *Blood Orange*

'A brilliantly-observed and compelling thriller.'
—Anna Mazzola, author of *The Story Keeper*

'A roller coaster read, full of thrills and one spectacular spill!'
—Liz Nugent, bestselling author of *Skin Deep*

'*What You Did* is a triumph, a gripping story of the secrets and lies that can underpin even the closest friendships. Put some time aside – this is one you'll want to read in a single sitting.'
—Kevin Wignall, bestselling author of *A Death in Sweden* and *The Traitor's Story*

'Hitting the rare sweet spot between a satisfying read and a real page-turner, this brilliantly written book deserves to fly high.'
—Cass Green, bestselling author of *In a Cottage In a Wood*

'A meticulous thriller full of twists and false turns.'

—Crime Time

'Creepy and oh-so-clever.'

—*Fabulous*

'A fantastic and intense book that grips you right from the very first line.'

—*We Love This Book*

'McGowan's pacey, direct style ensures that the twists come thick and fast.'

—*The Irish Times*

'A riveting police thriller.'

—*Woman* (Pick of the Week)

'Taut plotting and assured writing.'

—*Good Housekeeping*

'You'll be desperate to know what happened and how everything will turn out.'

—*The Sun*

'An excellent murder mystery.'

—*Bella*

'Plenty of twists and turns keep you hooked.'

—*Crime Monthly*

THE VANISHING TRIANGLE

ALSO BY CLAIRE McGOWAN

THE VANISHING TRIANGLE

The Murdered Women Ireland Forgot

CLAIRE McGOWAN

Little
a

Published by Little A, New York

www.apub.com

Amazon, the Amazon logo, and Little A are trademarks of Amazon.com, Inc.,
or its affiliates.

ISBN-13: 9781542035293
ISBN-10: 1542035295

Cover design by kid-ethic

Printed in the United States of America

To all the missing and murdered women and
their families

NOTE

When I was growing up, just by the border near Newry, County Down, we called the place we lived 'Northern Ireland' or 'the North' – never 'Ulster', because Ulster means the whole nine counties of the original province, not the six that make up Northern Ireland. We called the rest of Ireland 'Southern Ireland', 'the South', or even 'down South'. We rarely called it 'the Republic of Ireland', and never 'Eire'. In Ireland, words are rarely straightforward, so although some people will prefer different terms, since this is what I've always called these places, I've done so in this book. I've also sometimes used the term 'police' for clarity, though they are of course called the Gardaí or Guards in Ireland. The police force in Northern Ireland at this time was the RUC, and is now called the PSNI, a changeover that happened in 2001.

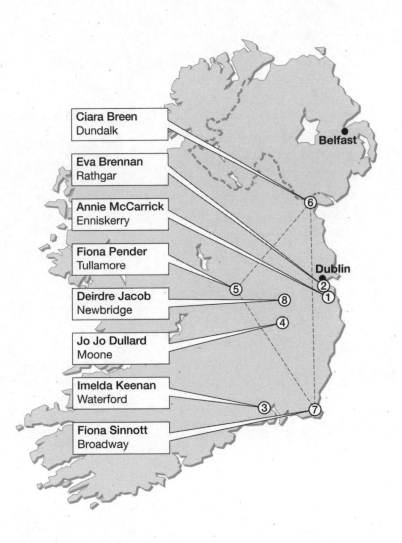

Ciara Breen
Dundalk

Eva Brennan
Rathgar

Annie McCarrick
Enniskerry

Fiona Pender
Tullamore

Deirdre Jacob
Newbridge

Jo Jo Dullard
Moone

Imelda Keenan
Waterford

Fiona Sinnott
Broadway

Belfast

Dublin

Prologue

Imagine this. You're a young woman in rural Ireland, the kind of place where bad things don't really happen. Close-knit communities, fresh air and green hills, *céad míle fáilte*. That's what you thought, anyway. But something has gone very wrong. Right now, you're in a story from another country. You're being held down on the floor of a car, pressed into the footwell of the passenger seat. A man you don't know has seized you off the street and thrown you into his car. He's driving around the dark lanes of rural Wicklow. He has raped you once already, in a remote field, and you can tell he's driving into the mountains now. He's got country and western music on the radio, he's humming along. You know, perhaps, that these mountains are notorious as a place to hide bodies. You know that in the nineties, eight women went missing in this small corner of Ireland, and several more were found murdered in the same area. You've seen his face, and he has spoken to you about his family, his life. You know what it means, that he's told you these things. That he didn't bother to hide his face.

The car stops. It's pitch-black where you are, not a sound, not a light, and you have no idea where you are. As he turns off the engine, you know he is going to kill you.

The crime I am thinking of took place in February 2000, on a dark and cold night in the centre of Carlow, a small town in the south-east of Ireland. But equally I could be thinking of a more recent case, from 2018, where a young woman getting off a bus was snatched from the road in broad daylight – it was just after six on a May evening, and she was shoved into a Nissan Qashqai and driven away. The stories are so similar.

Life had moved on in Ireland in the eighteen years since the Carlow attack. The witness who saw the second abduction, a woman driving her child home, had a mobile phone so she could call the police right away. As soon as the Gardaí knew what make of car the attacker drove – from the witness and from CCTV on the bus the woman had stepped off – they tracked him down easily. They found his address, went to his door, had his wife call him on his mobile when he wasn't home. There was even CCTV of him walking to his car before the attack, after drinking in a pub earlier that evening. The Gardaí did everything they could with this knowledge. Helicopters, search parameters, roadblocks, number plate scans. A manhunt was launched. The next day, the suspect was shot in a stand-off with police, and died after taking a bullet to the shoulder. He left a bloodstained note saying where to find the woman. Frantically, the police searched for her, but she was already dead, raped and strangled. Her body was found the day after that, dumped in a patch of gorse. The Gardaí thought she'd been killed within forty-five minutes of her abduction. Her name was Jastine Valdez, and she was twenty-four years old.

You might think this sounds like an American story, from a land of lonely highways and armed cops, but in fact it happened near Dublin, Ireland, in a populated area and in broad daylight. And it wasn't even unusual. The worst part was – it had happened before. Possibly many times.

After this murder, people began to recall other, similar cases. The Carlow attack, of course, with such a similar MO, and others before that too. The missing women from the nineties, the dirty secret of Dublin and around. I've so far not come across anyone outside Ireland who's heard of these cases, but people there remember. Between 1993 and 1998, eight women went missing from an area roughly eighty miles around Dublin, leading some to nickname it the 'vanishing triangle'. There was speculation about a serial killer, responsible for some or all of these cases. It's worth noting that not everyone likes this name, or believes it was the same person who killed the women, although almost everyone agrees they must be dead. It's true that this is the most densely populated area of the country, and that over 9,000 people are reported missing each year in Ireland, with around 900 considered long-term missing. All the same, the population in the nineties was only 3.5 million, and so many disappearances so close to each other, with no bodies ever found, raise questions.

Was there in fact a serial killer at work in Ireland, never identified until it was too late? Despite the large number of disappearances in a short space of time, it was years before they were even examined together, and by then they had stopped. As well as the missing, there were also several murders during this time or just before, of women whose bodies were found in the same mountainous area. A connection between the disappearances has never been formally declared, and in most cases the women's families found the response from the Irish police disappointing and inadequate. A task force set up to look into the triangle disappearances, Operation Trace, failed to either link the cases or find any sign of the missing women. The youngest was seventeen. One was heavily pregnant when she disappeared. One was American, of Irish heritage. One went missing right outside her front door, in the middle of the day. All left behind families who've never had answers, or even a body to bury.

The 2018 murder of Jastine Valdez, so shocking and incomprehensible, stirred up all these questions again, memories of the missing and dead women from twenty years before, many of them possibly pulled into cars and abducted, or last seen walking along main roads. Jastine was even taken from the same village where the first missing woman was last seen, in 1993. Could these cases all be linked? Was this latest murder a resurgence in the same series of crimes?

When I heard about Jastine's murder in 2018, like many other Irish people I started thinking about the nineties cases. I was growing up in Ireland myself during this time, just north of the border. I was eleven when the first disappearance took place and sixteen when they ended, but I don't remember hearing anything about them at the time, no news reports, no warnings that women and girls were going missing. Although I was young I watched the news every night from the time I was in primary school, which is maybe something you do when you grow up in a war zone. I was two years younger than one of the missing women, one year younger than another. But I was never told their names. I don't remember advice to be careful, or not any more than the usual warnings that girls are given as soon as they can walk. Don't take a lift. Don't trust strangers. Don't wear that. Like it's your own responsibility. Instead, I first heard about the cases when I was almost thirty, researching a series of novels about a fictional missing persons unit. At the time I was shocked – how could so many women vanish and it was barely even talked about?

The 2018 murder stirred up memories for me too, and made me want to explore this question further. How *could* it happen? Why were all these cases unsolved, with no leads at all, no bodies ever found? Why wasn't there more outcry at the time, more fear? Eight suspicious disappearances in a small area of a small country, plus several murders and abductions with a similar MO, that's a lot. As I looked into it, I was shocked to find that Ireland has a big problem with missing persons, with a number of key recommendations still not implemented. Northern and Southern Ireland also don't work together as well as they could, especially given how easy it would be for a killer to cross the border. I decided I wanted more people to know about the older cases, and also to find out for myself what conditions had caused so many disappearances, with so little publicity. I wanted to understand how this kind of thing could happen in the country where I grew up, which I always felt was safe as long as you stayed away from politics.

I've always had an interest in crime. I remember being nine or ten and sneaking lurid, violent books from the shelves in my great-aunt's house. My aunt – who never married, went to mass every day, and would pointedly send me out of the room if something even vaguely risqué came on TV – was a huge true crime fan, and had a house stuffed with books about the Moors murders, 10 Rillington Place and other gruesome stories. So maybe that's where my interest came from. Or maybe it's no surprise, when you grow up in a country saturated with death and violence, that you would be drawn to the dark side. I always knew I wanted to be a novelist, and, as an adult, I naturally gravitated towards writing crime fiction. But I had never investigated real crimes before.

When I started working on this book, I was overwhelmed with feelings of inadequacy. Although I had known about these cases for years, I'm not a journalist and am not used to interviewing people or to investigating – I make up stories for a living. It seemed to me there were lots of men involved in the cases, a wall of male experts – journalists, detectives, politicians. I was very aware of my gender, my age (though at thirty-eight I'm not exactly young) and my lack of professional background. And yet I'm a woman not far in age from the missing ones, and I understand what it was like in the nineties, how easily you might take a lift with a stranger, or walk home along deserted roads. How hard it would have been to imagine that somewhere like Ireland, our homely little country where everyone knew your business, could have hidden a serial killer and no one even realised. I saw myself at that age and younger, riding my bike around the countryside alone, travelling to late-night discos twenty miles away, stopping to give directions to strangers who called to me from cars. I would have and did do all of these things. Had I been in danger all along and not realised?

I'm also writing as someone who usually deals in fiction. In the crime stories I write, we will always find the answers. We'll discover exactly what happened to the missing person, why they disappeared, if someone took them or if they ran away themselves. The guilty will be brought to justice, every time, and the bereaved will find some comfort. But in real life, it doesn't work like that. Things don't always have meaning, they just happen and we don't know why. A family man pulls a woman into his car and rapes her. A girl gets off a bus on a warm evening and her life ends forty-five minutes later. A woman runs to catch a bus on a spring afternoon and is never seen again. Another woman misses a bus and hitch-hikes home, with the same outcome. Killers go undetected, sometimes for ever. We live with the not-knowing.

In these cases, there's so much we don't know. There are no crime scenes, no bodies, very little evidence. In the nineties there wasn't even CCTV or mobile phone records, or the number plate recognition technology police can call on nowadays. The women are just gone, and I wasn't going to uncover new evidence that hadn't been seen before. A team of six Gardaí worked on the disappearances every day for three years and ultimately found nothing new. Besides, in-depth books about the cases already exist, written by crime journalists and even by a detective on the task force.

So, in the absence of concrete answers, I'm taking a different tack – I want to look at how and why so many women could go missing without a national outcry, without the disappearances even being linked for so long. Why, in so many of the cases, the same excuses were made for a disappearance: she'd been depressed, she must have killed herself; she'd had an abortion, she must have been unhappy; she'd had boyfriends, she must have gone off with a man. I also found cases where a chief suspect is very well known to police, but has never been charged, and even where violent men were convicted of crimes but released from prison a few years later, ready to reoffend. I wanted to find out why men who hurt women are so often protected and shielded by institutions. Why the police made so many mistakes. Ultimately, I wanted to know what kind of country Ireland really is. What kind of country allows crimes like this to happen? To ask, if it's possible to answer such a big question, *why*. Why do these terrible events occur? Inevitably, of course, I also have my own thoughts on possible suspects.

In this book, I'll look at a variety of different factors that perhaps contributed to these disappearances, and in some cases murders, and the fact that they remain unsolved to this day. I'll also look at a few cases that probably aren't linked to the triangle ones, but all the same tell us something important about why these crimes happened in Ireland. I can't offer a forensic solution, but I can talk about what it was like to be a young girl in Ireland in the nineties. I can talk about the political turmoil that masked so many other news stories. The secrecy and shame, especially around sex. The isolation of villages with little public transport, in the days before mobile phones and the internet. The way the justice system repeatedly protects violent men, at the expense of women and children.

It's important too to understand the context. These disappearances took place at a time of great change, in a country trying to drag itself out from centuries of misogyny and religious dogma. It wasn't until 1997 that divorce was legalised in Ireland, for example. It was illegal to be gay until 1993, a date that I always have to go back and check, because it can't be true, it just can't. It is, though. The last Magdalene Laundry, those abusive homes for pregnant girls, closed in 1996, although there was a mother and baby home open in Northern Ireland until at least 1998. And in 1992, the year before the first disappearance, a fourteen-year-old girl was placed under house arrest by the state, to stop her leaving Ireland to have an abortion. She had been raped by an older man who later went on to attack another young girl. In this climate, it's perhaps not surprising that police often failed to launch searches for the women for some time after they'd gone missing.

Another shocking news story in these years was the clerical abuse scandal, which shook the faith of Irish Catholics to its core. Father Brendan Smyth, a prolific paedophile who abused hundreds of children over the years, after being moved around from parish to parish each time he offended so it could be hushed up, was arrested in 1991. But due to the fact of the border, which at this stage both existed (in that it was real, a line on a map) and didn't exist (in that there was nothing there, no checkpoints or barriers – Schrödinger's border), he was able to simply cross over to Ireland from the North and stay there for three years, as the RUC in Northern Ireland desperately sought an extradition warrant. In so many cases, these men were protected by silence, by moving them quietly along when they committed crimes, so that more children and women could be hurt, more lives destroyed. It was not just the Church that did this, but also the IRA and even the state itself.

In the nineties, Ireland was also going through rapid economic change, officially joining the euro in 1999. After centuries of emigration, finally this was reversed, and even now almost 3 per cent of the population is from Poland alone. The Celtic Tiger – the name given to Ireland's booming economy at this time – meant lots of building work. Lots of places to hide a body. The bust in 2008 has left half-built ghost estates scattered around the countryside, a legacy of greed and over-speculation that couldn't last. Before this, though, the national mood was buoyant, with a sense that Ireland was taking its place on a world stage. We even won the Eurovision Song Contest four times in the nineties, and qualified for the World Cup twice. Are some of these Tiger-time properties, the hotels and luxury estates, hiding dark secrets in the foundations? Or did the disappearances perhaps not fit with people's view of Ireland as wealthy, successful, effervescent, and so they weren't given the attention they deserved? How else could so many women vanish and never be found, in a small country where everyone knows everyone? It seems unbelievable no trace of them has ever surfaced.

At the time of these disappearances, the news was also full of the Northern Irish Troubles, and the shaky progress of the peace process between 1994 (the year of the first ceasefires, which eventually broke down two years later with a huge bomb in London's Canary Wharf) and 1998, when the Good Friday Agreement was signed. It's long been speculated that the strain on police forces both north and south of the border led to non-sectarian crimes, especially against women, being overlooked. Ordinary murders, you might call them. Growing up, we always had the impression this kind of thing didn't happen in Ireland. If you were going to be killed, it would be by a stray bullet or a bomb going off. Not being snatched by a stranger off the road. Except it did happen, of course – it turns out a rural Irish childhood was not as safe as I had thought.

◆ ◆ ◆

The eight missing vanishing triangle women usually grouped together are:

Annie McCarrick, twenty-six: an American of Irish heritage, who was last seen running for a bus to go for a walk in the Wicklow

Hills in 1993. She was expecting dinner guests the next day, who arrived to find her gone and food left out to spoil.

Eva Brennan, thirty-nine: she also disappeared in 1993 after a family lunch ended in a row, but despite this out-of-character action, the Gardaí failed to investigate her case for three months.

Imelda Keenan, twenty-two: Imelda went missing on her way to the post office, in the middle of the day on the busy streets of Waterford town, at the start of 1994.

Jo Jo Dullard, twenty-one: she vanished while hitching home in the middle of the night in late 1995. She rang a friend from a phone box, only to say she had a lift and rush off.

Fiona Pender, twenty-five: Fiona went missing in 1996, when she was almost eight months pregnant, last seen in her own home.

Ciara Breen, seventeen: Ciara lived in the neighbouring town to mine, just over the border. She went missing in 1997, from her own bedroom in the middle of the night.

Fiona Sinnott, nineteen: a young mother with a baby, she was also last seen in her own home in 1998, which was later found to have been cleaned and stripped of her belongings.

Deirdre Jacob, eighteen: Deirdre lived in London, where she was at teacher training college, and had just come home for the holidays. She vanished within sight of her own front door, at 3 p.m. in the middle of a summer's day in 1998.

After this the disappearances seemed to stop – no one knows why.

They are a random mix of women, of different ages and different backgrounds, with no apparent common ground or connection between them, which in itself is a little unusual, given how small Ireland is. I'm always surprised that, when I talk about this project, people's first question is, 'Were they sex workers?' (though usually they don't use this term). Think about what it means, that question – that we expect a certain type of woman to go missing, to be murdered. Not women like us. Perhaps what this question means is, if women like us went missing, and so many of them in a row, surely there would be a scandal, an investigation blazed across every newspaper and TV screen. But this was Ireland, in a time just before mobile phones, before widespread CCTV (which would only be found in banks and maybe shopping centres at this point), in the infancy of DNA science. And in Ireland, despite the gossip and tittle-tattle of small towns, people keep quiet about the big things.

There are others missing too, women who somehow fell through the cracks in these years. Arlene Arkinson, for example, who was fifteen when she went missing in Northern Ireland in 1994. She's not usually included in the list of triangle women because she lived in a different part of the country. But should we draw the line for that reason? There is so much we don't know about the eight cases, including whether they were linked at all, and, if so, whether the same person was responsible. And if there was one killer, had that person perhaps attacked women before, but less successfully? It's very common for serial killers to have earlier victims, ones who survived, or to have committed murders that weren't covered up as well. If you murder someone and make it look as if they aren't dead, as if they just walked away from their life, how much easier for you. But what if your first killings were less planned, less competent – what if you left a trail those times?

When the Gardaí began to draw links between the cases, they were also aware that the same area around Dublin had seen quite a few murders of women in the years before the nineties. There are at least four that may be connected, women whose bodies turned up in the Wicklow Mountains, in some cases just a few miles from each other. I think it's important to look at these too, as there's a high chance they are connected to the disappearances, perhaps the first attempts of a killer who later got better at hiding his crimes. I'll also include some cases from other parts of Ireland, such as Arlene's.

This is because I think the border has been used as an excuse too often – a way to let guilty men escape, to wash hands of responsibility, pretend that a determined predator could not have simply driven over a line on a map that by the late eighties was barely even manned. The whole concept of the vanishing triangle is invented, after all, an attempt to impose meaning on these occurrences. If there was a single killer, they would not necessarily have confined themselves to one part of the country. But which is worse – one killer or several? To think a serial murderer was out there all this time, not even recognised let alone caught, or that Ireland, our lovely welcoming country, awash with Guinness and craic, is also full of predators?

So what happened to the woman I mentioned first, abducted from Carlow in 2000? A successful businesswoman in her late twenties, who ran her own clothes shop, she locked up around half six in the evening, bringing with her the day's takings of some £700. She then walked across the nearby car park, heading to her vehicle, when a man suddenly appeared out of the darkness and attacked her, shoved her into her own passenger seat and drove the short distance to his own car, which was parked out of sight. This all happened within minutes. He made her take her shoes off, perhaps to stop her running away. He punched her, lightning-quick, breaking her nose. He made her undress, then tied her hands with her bra, and shoved a Gaelic football headband into her mouth to silence her, then put her in the seat beside him, pressing her head down near the gear stick. He drove away.

After a while he stopped, in a muddy field in the middle of nowhere, and dragged her out of the car. He raped her. Afterwards he pushed her into the boot and drove off again. It was barely half past eight in the evening at this point, but no one saw any of it. She lay in the boot of his car, noticing an aerosol can of something rattling around in the space beside her, as well as a small football like a child might play with. She'd already seen there was a child's seat in the car – he had kids, he'd said, two boys. He even told her their names and ages, making her even more terrified, because she knew what that meant.

In the Wicklow Mountains, an isolated and dark spot, he stopped for a second time. This was her chance. When he opened the boot, she sprayed the aerosol – a kind of paint – right into his face, but it didn't work and nothing came out. She'd lost her only chance to save herself. He raped her again in the car, several times, reclining the driver's seat to do it, so she could see the baby seat in the back; he was attacking her in the same car he drove his children around in. Then, in this clearing in the woods, he put a plastic bag over her head, and began to strangle her. She managed somehow to break free and she ran – but she couldn't see anything in the dark with the bag on her head, and she stumbled into barbed wire. She was caught. Trapped. It was over. She was dead.

But the story wasn't finished yet. Just then she saw a glaring light filling the clearing. She heard male voices. What was this – more men come to hurt her? This woman was minutes, maybe seconds, from death, staggering across the remote clearing, tangled in wire, on a cold winter's night miles from anywhere. It was pure blind luck that anyone was there at all. The two men who'd found her were hunters out 'lamping', a practice that means using lights attached to guns to scare small animals into freezing, so they can be shot more easily. Instead of prey, they'd picked up the woman in the powerful lights attached to their weapons, and ran to help her, while her abductor drove off at speed. The woman was deranged with fear, no idea where she was or what was happening to her. It took her a while to understand she was safe. She wasn't going to die that night after all. She would live.

It was such a choreographed attack, so fast and so brutal. The man knew how to drive with her in the car, head pressed down so no one could see her. He knew not to drag her even the short distance across the car park to his own vehicle, but to drive her car over to it instead. He used her own clothes to tie her up, maybe so he wouldn't be caught with what the police sometimes call a 'rape kit' – items like ropes, knives, blindfolds, gags. His children's toys were in the car, maybe to make him look innocent, a family man. He knew where to take her so they wouldn't be disturbed – and it was only a huge fluke that they were. It was hard to believe he'd never done this before.

Ireland is a small place. One of the hunters, it turned out, knew the man who'd run from the clearing; a while previously, he had groped the hunter's friend in a local pub. It later transpired this man had also tried to touch his own wife's best friend when he gave her a lift home one night, but nothing else had ever surfaced about him, nothing criminal, and the woman hadn't told anyone, because this was her friend's husband, a decent man. Wasn't he? The kind of man that several women might have had bad vibes about, or perhaps an uncomfortable run-in with, that later they would talk themselves out of, sure that they were mistaken or overreacting.

The hunters took the woman to the local Garda station, where they explained who they'd seen. Several hours later, a thirty-five-year-old carpenter named Larry Murphy returned to his home, looked in on his sleeping children and slid into bed with his wife. All appeared normal. But the next day, Larry Murphy was arrested for abducting the woman in Carlow. He didn't even try to hide it – the men in the clearing had seen him, and he'd seen them. He handed over the money he'd stolen from the woman, the takings from her clothes shop, and said: '*I don't know why I did it.*'

On 17 February 2000, Larry Murphy was brought to court and charged. In the dock he wore a fleece and jeans, and stared at the floor, not speaking. He had never been convicted of anything before, never even been arrested. But it seemed clear from the savagery and speed of the attack that this was not the first time he'd done it, and that except for that one twist of luck, the woman he'd taken would not have survived the night. Here was a man who knew how to abduct women, operating in the same area where so many others had gone missing. Was this the killer Gardaí had been looking for? Was he responsible for the disappearances between 1993 and 1998? That, unfortunately, is the end of that part of the story. With no bodies and no hard evidence, Murphy has never admitted to or been convicted of any other crime, and he got out of prison in 2010 – five years less than he was sentenced to. The disappearances went unsolved and neglected for another eight years, when Jastine Valdez's murderer surfaced.

The unnamed Carlow woman was lucky, if we can use that word for surviving a brutal rape and attempted murder. She lived through the night, against the odds, and her attacker was caught and imprisoned. Jastine Valdez did not survive when the same thing happened to her. She was a young and beautiful student, a representation of modern Ireland, post-Celtic Tiger, a diverse and tolerant Ireland. She had lived in Dublin for three years, coming to study and join her Filipino parents, who'd been working there since the 1990s. The man who took her, just like Larry Murphy, was a husband and father with two children, who had never before been on the Gardaí's radar, had no convictions, gave no sign that he would ever do anything like this. He was most likely a stranger to Jastine, though police thought it was possible he'd seen her before and had been stalking her. She was going about her life, on a normal day, when she was pulled into a car, raped and murdered. Had this man – Mark Hennessy was his name – done it before? Maybe in the nineties? Was *he* the triangle killer who may or may not have existed? Unfortunately, as he was shot by police the day after he took Jastine, that question remains unanswered. Later I'll look at the evidence against both men, as well as several other possible suspects.

Jastine was murdered in 2018. It was the year Ireland repealed the Eighth Amendment and legalised abortion – in fact just six days after Jastine's death. The year after it elected a gay Prime Minister with immigrant parents. It was also the year that a rape trial was held in Belfast – one where the court saw text messages the men, professional rugby players, had sent to each other, laughing about what happened and using words like pumping, roasting, and sluts. Although they were acquitted, the case stirred up a maelstrom of misogyny, and the woman involved was doxxed – that is, her name made public online – and the man who did it fined only £300. She wept in court, as the barrister asked why she hadn't screamed, pointed out that there were 'middle-class' girls downstairs who would have helped her, even though some of those girls were passed out drunk. So much misogyny was released by that case that some Irish men reportedly were planning to vote no in the abortion referendum, just to 'get back' at women in general. Think of the depths of hatred that invokes. To say, I want you, a stranger, to have to carry an unwanted baby or make the trip back from England, bleeding and sore, because I am angry a famous man I don't know was accused, and not even convicted of rape.

2018 was also the year of another rape case in Ireland, a seventeen-year-old attacked on a country lane, where the girl's pants were held up in court and the jury was asked whether a woman who wasn't up for it would really wear something like this. It was the year when another young woman – just fourteen this time – was found murdered, stripped naked, tortured, in an abandoned house not far from her home, an attack that again took place in broad daylight on a summer's evening, only two weeks before Jastine Valdez was murdered. It was the year when over 4,000 women from both North and South Ireland made the trip to England to end pregnancies, knowing that at home to even buy abortion pills online could get you sent to prison. The following year, a woman in Northern Ireland (let's not forget, part of the UK) faced jail for buying abortion pills online for her teenage daughter. This is our modern Ireland. The progress that we've made since the nineties is real, but it's not enough, not yet. As well as Jastine's murder, a lot of other events occurred in 2018 and 2019 that were relevant to these triangle cases. Arrests were made. Bogs and fields were searched, foundations dug up. Suspects emerged. Relatives died, still with no answers. So now seems like a good time to revisit the stories of these missing women, in the hope that their names can be kept alive.

What does it even mean to be missing? In most cases, someone knows where you are, even if it's only your abductor, your killer. If you've gone away voluntarily, are you still missing? Who are you missing to, exactly? This type of case is hard. There is no body, often no forensics, no DNA, no crime scene, nothing. Gardaí can only wait for a body to turn up some day, or for someone to talk. Or for that person to return, which seems so unlikely that most of the families have accepted their daughters are dead. But on the other hand, long-missing people have sometimes returned alive, years after being lost. In some ways this must be the cruellest thing of all – the terrible persistence of hope.

Chapter One

Then: Five Murders

The first disappearance in the triangle took place in March 1993. But to really understand the context, we have to look before that. Ireland in the eighties and nineties was a place of turmoil, change, confusion. I started at convent school in Northern Ireland in 1993, aged eleven. What I most recall about a Northern Irish childhood at this time is the simultaneous feeling of safety and danger. On the one hand, I lived in a small village where everyone knew each other, and it was considered safe for me to walk home alone from the age of ten, and let myself in with a key. We weren't worried about being abducted by strangers in cars – what we worried about was being accidentally shot by the soldiers who crouched in the hedgerows as we walked home. They were just a normal sight, boys often not much older than us, in camouflage gear with guns in their hands. Usually we ignored each other, but I'd hold my body tense as I passed, afraid to breathe.

We had good reason to be scared of them – I remember at least two occasions in the nineties where teenagers were shot by soldiers, in 1990 and 1992. And of course we were afraid of being killed by the terrorists, caught up in a bomb blast or hit by a stray bullet. This happened to children all the time – for example the Warrington bombings of 1993 (just a week before the first disappearance), then the Shankill Road chip shop bomb the same year. One day in April 1989, when I was seven, a bomb went off at the police station in Warrenpoint, the next town over from where I lived, just two miles away. A young woman, Joanne Reilly, was working in the hardware shop next door; she was twenty years old, and a Catholic, not that it matters. She died when the bomb went off. The IRA was sorry – it had meant to give a warning but something had gone wrong. In their world view, this was just an unfortunate accident. The same police station was bombed again as recently as 2014 – luckily no one was hurt this time, but it shows that the violence is not exactly over.

That summer, we didn't want to go out to play. We knew there was danger in the quiet country lanes. When we drove into the big town – Newry, ten miles away – we passed the memorial for soldiers blown up in 1979, two years before I was born. Even in my own tiny village, Rostrevor, two police officers had been shot in the street outside the post office in 1983. I don't remember this, but I knew it had happened. Rostrevor is two streets, nine pubs, pretty mountains, an annual folk-music festival. It's not somewhere things like this should happen. Newry police station, just around the corner from what would be my secondary school, was attacked with a mortar in 1985. Nine people died, the youngest nineteen years old. Two of them were Catholics. The violence was ever-present.

In many ways, being a girl was not a barrier in Ireland in the nineties. My convent school pushed us to study hard, be as good as the boys in their school across town. Our parents had been taught that Northern Irish Catholics would only rise up if they found professional jobs. They had also, more subtly, been taught that outbreeding the Protestants would one day tip the balance and perhaps lead to a united Ireland, and maybe this was true – the demographics are about to shift any day now in favour of a Catholic majority, as early as 2021 by some predictions, and who knows what will happen with Brexit. Some of our mothers didn't work, true, but others, like my own, had professional, well-paid jobs.

On the other hand, there was so much sexual shame around, so much silence about our bodies, so much secret abuse. People married young and had big families: six children was the norm at my school. The truth about paedophile priests was starting to come out, a challenge to everything we'd been taught about respecting the clergy, obeying the Church even when it seemed ridiculous. At the time I raged against what I saw as religious propaganda, and summed up the general attitude we were taught as: don't have sex, but if you do, don't use contraception because it's against God's will. And if you do that and get pregnant, definitely don't have an abortion as that is a major sin. Our 'family planning' education took place as part of religion class, which says it all really. Despite this woeful dereliction of duty, there were very few pregnancies at my school, mostly because everyone was so thoroughly terrified of sinning. Women's rights, or the lack of them, and the level of protection children and women could expect from the state, were very much on the agenda going into the nineties. Ireland was a country in the grip of painful change, trying to prise off the fingers of Church control, struggling with its self-identification as one of the few true Catholic countries left. Not everyone wanted to live that way anymore, or put up with the hypocrisy of punishing women for straying, when men, even the men in charge of the Church, were allowed to get away with it.

◆ ◆ ◆

Despite all the violence and the all-pervading sense of shame, we felt safe in other ways as children. We rode our bikes for miles, ran in and out of each other's gardens on long summer nights as darkness slowly fell. Adults would speak to you while you were out and about, and it would be considered rude not to reply. Often, they knew your name, and talked as if you ought to recognise them, or they'd say they knew your parents. It was common to offer and take lifts, and to pick up hitch-hikers. I lived at the end of a curved cul-de-sac of bungalows, one street branching off into two and beyond that, only fields. I played with the girl next door and the one across the street; Kerbies, Mother May I, Grandmother's Footsteps, although we didn't call it that. I can't remember what we called it. The only cars that drove into our street, apart from the few residents, had usually lost their way and were looking for a place to turn around. I went to a primary school even further into the countryside, which still had open fires and outdoor loos, and where, on summer days, we would be let out early to roam the fields near the school, picking dandelions and dodging sheep poo. There were ten children in my class, including me. A war was going on around us, yes, but life was mostly quiet, even boring.

So there it was, a safe and a dangerous place at the same time. However, as I began to find out when I started researching, Ireland was not as safe as it seemed during this time. In fact, there were a handful of brutal murders during my childhood, most unsolved to this day, that could very well be linked to the later disappearances.

Going back as far as 1979, a woman vanished from the town of Newbridge, about thirty miles from Dublin, where the final disappearance would also take place in 1998. Phyllis Murphy, who was twenty-three, went missing on 22 December while out shopping; as we go on we'll see how many of these disappearances occur around Christmas. She was last seen walking to the bus stop, around 7 p.m., wearing jeans and a winter coat, mittens. It's likely her killer gave her a lift in his car then drove her out into the mountains, beating her savagely before raping her. Gardaí thought she had tried to run from him, since the Christmas presents she'd bought for her family were found scattered around the nearby area. Her other possessions were dumped in different places, her clothes set on fire by the side of the road. Her body was found almost a month later, in a forest in Wicklow. She had been raped and strangled. In a harbinger of a later case in 1995, the cold temperatures at this time of year would preserve her body, and eventually condemn her killer, though not for two decades and not until DNA testing was in common use. This man got away with what he'd done for twenty years. What were the chances he'd killed Phyllis, dumped her body like rubbish, then lived a blameless life for another two decades? After his arrest, in 1999, there were no more disappearances. Was that just a coincidence? In 1979, however, the leads dried up and Phyllis's murder remained unsolved. Although this case seems far outside the scope of the disappearances – fourteen years before the first missing woman it shows that killers may strike once then either never do it again, or be more careful about leaving a trail.

A few years later, in 1982, Patricia Furlong, who was twenty, was strangled at a music festival held not far from Johnnie Fox's pub in Glencullen village, near Dublin, which would become significant in the first disappearance in 1993. Her body was left in a field, not even hidden, and hundreds of people were in the area where she was murdered. In this case, Gardaí had a chief suspect, a man facing countless allegations of violence against women both before and after Patricia's death, but weren't able to convict him until 1991. He was in prison until 1995, when he got out on appeal, and died in 1998, the year of the last disappearances. That meant he wasn't around for most of the triangle disappearances, but he was for these earlier murders. Assuming he did kill Patricia after all, did he do it again in the nineties and manage not to get caught this time?

There was also Antoinette Smith, in 1987 – there are no suspects at all in her murder. She was twenty-seven, the mother of two young girls, separated amicably from her husband. He minded the kids while she went off with a friend to a David Bowie concert at Slane Castle, then into Dublin to go drinking. She had left her friend around two in the morning, when Antoinette wanted to stay out and the friend didn't. The friend gave her a key, said to let herself in when she came back. She never did. A Dublin taxi driver said he'd picked up a woman who sounded like Antoinette that night, along with two men, taking them a few miles out of town towards a place called Rathfarnham. That's also a town that would feature in later cases. The men had given him an uncomfortable feeling, the driver said, making jokes about killing him and taking the car. Police weren't able to work out who these men might have been, or if that was even Antoinette with them.

No one was ever caught for murdering Antoinette, and her body wasn't found for almost a year, buried in bog land near Glencree, County Wicklow. This is very close to Enniskerry, which is where Jastine Valdez was abducted, and also where the first triangle disappearance took place in 1993. When she was found, she had plastic bags over her head, just like Larry Murphy had done to the woman in Carlow. Larry Murphy was in his early twenties in 1987 – could he have committed this terrible crime, or is it just coincidence again? Antoinette was identified by the wig she wore, having suffered from alopecia for years, and by her T-shirt from the Bowie concert, as well as her friend's door key, still in her pocket. Her younger daughter was four when she died. In 2019 her daughters – Lisa and Rachel – launched a new appeal for information. They haven't forgotten their mother, even though her death was over thirty years ago, and they think her murder was planned, not opportunistic, that she knew her killer. There were two men in the taxi with her, if that indeed was Antoinette. Had they known her beforehand? Did they do this together? Were some of the murders and disappearances perhaps a joint act?

The next murder was that of Inga Hauser, a young German woman who got off the ferry in Larne, in Northern Ireland, in 1988. It's not in the vanishing triangle, but a fact I'll keep coming back to is that Ireland isn't very big – only 300 miles at its longest point; there's nothing to suppose a determined killer wouldn't be prepared to drive over the border in search of prey, especially given the border barely existed by then. Inga was eighteen but brave and independent; she planned to backpack around Ireland and had been in Scotland beforehand. There were always German back-packers and caravanners in Ireland, even during the worst years, when there was no investment or tourist infrastructure, nowhere decent to eat. They still came, from their own divided country – maybe they imagined Ireland was a safe and unspoiled place. No one knows what happened to Inga after she got off the ferry, or if she met someone on board, got talking to them, took a lift, but her body was found in woodlands near Ballycastle two weeks later. Ballycastle is near where my mother grew up, a pretty seaside town with a famous ice-cream parlour – not the kind of place murders like this happen. Police also found her camera, with film in it. In a novel I would write, there'd be a clue in this, but the film was developed and only showed photos of her trip through Scotland. Inga had been raped, hit over the head, and her neck was broken. In many of these cases the women had been strangled, but to actually break a neck takes great force, and could suggest someone with some form of combat training. There were of course many soldiers in Northern Ireland at this time. There was movement on this case too in 2018 – someone was arrested (unnamed as yet), but so far nothing else has come of it. Still, it's encouraging to see that these cold cases, thirty years old now, aren't forgotten.

Other names, other women. Another Patricia, Patricia Doherty, who was out buying Christmas presents for her kids on 23 December 1991. Patricia was thirty, and was last seen, much like Phyllis Murphy back in 1979, waiting at a bus stop at around 9 p.m. (in Ireland it's common for shops to stay open till midnight just before Christmas). She'd been shopping in the town of Tallaght, and she went home briefly then popped back out again for some final items. Patricia's mother lived in Rathfarnham – only four miles from Tallaght, and the same place Antoinette Smith might have been going when last seen in 1987. Rathfarnham is also half an hour's drive from Newbridge, where Phyllis Murphy was last seen, which gives an idea of how these cases clustered together. Patricia was a prison officer, so when she wasn't home on Christmas Eve her husband thought he'd got mixed up about her shifts (no mobile phones at this time, of course – most people in Ireland didn't have mobiles until the end of the decade).

I find it interesting that several of these disappearances or murders took place near Christmas – does it bring out the violence in people? Or was the same person often out hunting at this time of year? Or just another coincidence? Patricia's body was eventually uncovered six months later in the bog, by a man cutting turf at a place called Lemass Cross, less than a mile from where Antoinette Smith's body had been left. Some clothes and jewellery were buried a distance away, showing that she hadn't ended up there by accident. No one was ever caught for killing Patricia, and there were never any real leads in either her case or Antoinette's. The pathologist thought she'd been strangled, but couldn't say for sure. Since her clothes were still on, the police at least hoped she hadn't been raped, though they couldn't be sure about that either. Small comfort.

So that's five murders in the years before the disappearances, four of them in the same triangle area where the missing women vanished. All unsolved for years, four of them still so. No links between the victims. All of them likely strangled and probably raped. I hardly need to say I hadn't heard about any of these murders before I started to look into them as an adult. Was that because I lived in Northern Ireland, and we act as if the border is a real barrier? Maybe, although I didn't know about the murder in the North either, even though I used to visit Ballycastle often as a child, because my granny lived near there. Again, I want to ask – what does it mean, that these killings happened? In one of my novels it would mean that the killer – because there would only be one, to tie things up neatly – had started earlier, with some sloppy murders, only to learn as he went on how to hide a body, how to make it look like a woman ran away from her life. Certainly, there are parallels between these murders, as well as with the cases in the nineties: Christmas disappearances; women last seen at bus stops, who might have accepted an offered lift; bodies buried in bog land in the Wicklow Mountains; strangulation; the same towns and villages cropping up repeatedly.

Was the same person already targeting women before the nineties cases? Did he learn from the investigations into those murders not to leave a body the next time? In real life, things aren't as neat as in novels, and we still don't know the answer to any of these questions. It is significant that, even with bodies and crime scenes and possessions left out for anyone to find, only one of these murders has been officially solved, and even then the killer was free for twenty years before DNA evidence and a tenacious police officer led to his arrest. And even when someone was convicted, as they were for Patricia Furlong's murder – though not for nine years in that case – he was freed on appeal after just four years. So perhaps it's not surprising Gardaí were never able to solve the later cases: there was no evidence at all. Did one of these men kill the women in the nineties, or were there several murderers operating in the triangle area at the same time? Is the violent death of women actually more common in Ireland than we'd like to admit? Maybe I'd been stupid to feel safe, to wander freely about the countryside as a child and young girl.

So this was the context of the nineties disappearances, which began in 1993. A country in the throes of change. Political turmoil, violence, sexual abuse scandals, massive social upheaval. A place thought of as safe, but where women were in fact already being murdered. These five murders left motherless children, grieving parents and husbands. Eventually the cases went cold, and hope dwindled. It was bad. It was about to get worse.

Chapter Two

TRANSPORT

Annie McCarrick was the first woman to vanish, in March 1993. Of all the missing women in Ireland during the nineties, Annie's disappearance is perhaps the most high profile. Maybe because, despite her all-Irish name, she was American, from Long Island, or perhaps because she was so clearly beautiful, happy, loved by so many. She was crazy about Ireland, and had been living in Dublin for several months when she went missing. Previously, she had studied English Literature there for three years, at Maynooth, a religious university near Dublin. She'd made a lot of friends, and had a relationship that had ended amicably. Annie was well settled in Dublin this second time, with local friends, and she'd arranged to have the brother of her ex-boyfriend and his fiancée, a couple named Hilary and Rita, round for dinner the day after she was last seen. Annie also had a job in a café, and as part of her work used to make desserts to sell.

Her last movements have to be guessed at, reconstructed from vague sightings in a world before widespread CCTV, but it's thought that on Friday, 26 March 1993, her day off, she decided to go to a place called Enniskerry for a walk (this is where Jastine

Valdez would be murdered in 2018, about fifteen miles from the centre of Dublin). It's a well-known beauty spot in the Wicklow Mountains, which within a few years would become synonymous with missing and dead women. Her birthday had been a few days before, and her mother was due to visit the following week; Annie had bought theatre tickets for them, which were found in her room when police searched it. Life seemed to be going well.

That morning, Annie said goodbye to her flatmates, who were visiting their families for the weekend. They said she was sitting up in bed knitting, something she enjoyed. She did some laundry, hand-washed delicates. She went out, bought groceries for the dinner, including cream and butter. She called in to a bank to switch her account to the local branch – the security camera caught the last definite sighting of her. Long curly hair, an ankle-length skirt. She glances towards the camera briefly, as if she knows it's there. She looks very young, full of life. Such an ordinary day, and yet everything she did in those hours takes on significance, because she was never seen again. So what happened to her after her brief appearance on that camera? Gardaí were able to trace her movements so far, then no further. We know Annie made a phone call to a friend, asking if she wanted to go for a walk – but the friend had hurt her ankle, so had to say no. Gardaí wondered if she had called someone else, a man maybe, but despite tests on the phone they weren't able to find evidence of another call.

Around 3.30 p.m., another friend from a previous job, Eimear O'Grady, said she saw Annie running for a bus, the number 44. Eimear was on the top deck of that bus, and as it was packed, she couldn't catch Annie's attention, but she was sure it was her. Annie was wearing cowboy boots, she said, and a tweed skirt. Being late for the bus could explain why Annie's bag of food was later found abandoned inside the door of the flat, the cream and butter going off. Would she have left it there until she came back, if she knew she was about to miss the only bus that hour? Was there someone she wanted to meet? She almost missed the bus as it was and had to run, but, this being Ireland, the driver stopped to let her on. It's one of those split-second *Sliding Doors* moments (a film that came out in 1998) that a whole life hinges on. If she hadn't caught the bus, if it had pulled away, as a London bus surely would have in the same situation, if she'd been a second or two later and the driver hadn't seen her, would she be alive now? If her friend hadn't injured her ankle and had gone with her, would Annie be here today, would no one outside her family and friends know her name? Would she be married, have children, still be living in Ireland or back in New York? The questions, the what-ifs, are haunting. Annie got off the bus in Ranelagh, where you would change if you wanted to go to Enniskerry. Her friend Eimear, still on the top deck, watched her disembark, and disappear.

No one quite knows what happened to her after that. There was a suggestion she might have bought stamps at the post office in Enniskerry, but the Gardaí couldn't confirm that she'd posted anything that day. Someone fitting her description was seen that night at Johnnie Fox's pub, a live music venue up in the hills, four miles from Enniskerry, and the same place where Patricia Furlong, one of the earlier women, had been murdered in 1982. Could Annie really have walked all the way there, in the dark? Famously, it's the highest pub in Ireland. It hosted an Irish dance show that might have appealed to someone like Annie, who loved the culture of the country. She had been there before, certainly, with her flatmates Eda and Jill.

The doorman at the pub, Sam Doran, said he thought Annie was there that night. He said he told her there was a cover charge of two punts (this was in pre-euro days), and she reached into her bag half-heartedly, as if expecting someone else to pay. If it was Annie, she was with a man, who paid for her. It was not clear if she knew the man already, or if he'd simply come up and offered to pay for her. This man, the doorman said, bought Annie drinks all night. He was wearing a waxed jacket, something like a Barbour – the word 'yuppie' was used. Clean-shaven, strong, a square face. A photofit of this man – with a large chin and nose – was issued. If this was Annie, maybe that man was her killer. Nobody knows and, before CCTV and mobile phones, we can only guess.

When I met Alan Bailey, a retired Garda who worked on the task force to find the women, I asked did he think that was Annie at Johnnie Fox's. He said he did, although at first he had been sceptical. The witnesses were simply too credible, he said, too consistent to ignore. For some reason, several of the staff had noticed Annie and the man with her – maybe there was something about the situation that made them remember it, some back-of-the-neck frisson of danger.

The following night, Saturday, 27 March, Annie's guests came round for dinner, but found no one there. Puzzled, they didn't know what to do. Annie did have a landline, although as Alan Bailey pointed out to me, not everyone did at this time, but her friends didn't know the number, so they called her mother Nancy in New York, which sparked a worry that would never calm. Lacking any other option, and since her mother knew nothing either, they went home.

The next day, Sunday, Annie didn't show up to work at the café or to collect her wages. Her flatmates returned home from their weekends away to find her gone, the groceries left out to go off. The ironing board was also out, and her flatmate said the telephone book was too, as if Annie had been looking up a number. The mess seemed odd for such a conscientious person. Did she not have time to tidy up? Was she meeting someone? A last-minute plan when her friend couldn't go walking with her? I know from living abroad myself several times that the weekends and days off can

32

be desperately lonely when you don't know many people. Perhaps Annie, feeling alone, and having just celebrated a birthday, reached out to someone she didn't know that well. It's what you do when you're trying to meet people and make friends. You know it's potentially dangerous, but you're lonely so you take the risk. When Annie hadn't appeared by Sunday night, her friends called her parents, Nancy and John, and told them the terrible news – she was missing.

Annie's father had been a cop in New York. When she didn't get in touch, he knew something was wrong. Her mother changed her flight and came to Ireland early to join the search. It broke her parents. If you raise your daughter in New York, dangerous and crime-ridden in the nineties, surely you don't expect her to go to Ireland, land of leprechauns and craic, and vanish there. You expect her to be safe. Her parents eventually divorced, as so many do when they lose a child, and John McCarrick died in 2009, only in his sixties. It's a common and heartbreaking theme in many of these cases, that the parents of the missing simply can't go on, broken by the years of uncertainty and pain. So often they die before their time, in their fifties and sixties. Annie was at least looked for, unlike some of the other women, but the trail eventually went cold. The FBI even got involved in her case at one stage, but still nothing has ever been found. Those are the last sightings of her: definitely in the bank, almost certainly on the bus, and quite probably in the pub with a man.

Bizarrely, however, there were reports a few months later that she was alive and living in Wicklow. A private investigator hired by her parents seemed to believe this, and said in the press that she 'had her own reasons' for not coming forward, which seems highly unlikely. Why would she do that to her family, her friends? Why would she leave her life without so much as putting her cream into the fridge? Why would she vanish when her mother was visiting soon, and she had the theatre tickets in her room? I'd love to know the reasons for thinking she might be alive, which it seems to me are based on nothing more than showing a video of her to several people in the area, who thought it was her.

There is quite a lot of information available about Annie's disappearance, and it's unusual in that her trail leads quite far, all the way to Johnnie Fox's pub in the mountains. I also found that in 2015, a documentary about Annie's case was shown on Irish TV. Although it's interesting and comprehensive, it really struck me while watching it how a female crime expert casually remarks that 'of course' Annie shouldn't have gone walking alone in the countryside. Watching in 2019, I bridled: why shouldn't she have? Shouldn't a woman be able to go wherever she wants, whenever she wants? Yes, it would have been getting dark within hours, in Ireland at three o'clock in March, but what are you supposed to do in winter in a cold country? Never leave the house? It wasn't even four o'clock when she set out. This throwaway comment made me think about how we judge women, how we are blamed for our own rapes and murders. There was a feeling in the media reports that Annie, a young woman abroad, raised near New York, had no sense of danger in Ireland. She loved the place, and had found the people so friendly, was so enamoured of the culture. I think there's something to that: in another country you may let your guard down, or do things you wouldn't do at home simply because you want to meet people. But who can blame her if she felt that way? I grew up in the Irish countryside and had little sense of danger either, outside the Troubles anyway.

As I read through news reports on the case, I realised there was an undercurrent of slight judgement. Annie had gone off by herself, perhaps to meet a man (though we have no proof of that). Maybe she'd accepted a lift, which explains how she travelled the four miles to the pub, as it would have been dark outside by that time. She had drunk with a strange man in a pub, let him pay for her, and since she had to get home to the city somehow, perhaps she had taken a lift back there as well. She had been walking in the countryside alone – is that enough to put you in danger? When I was a child – I was eleven when Annie went missing – I regularly went off on my own, roaming about our village and even further into the country. I walked and rode my bike, sometimes for miles, and I enjoyed being in nature by myself. If I was allowed to do this while still at primary school – and my parents were on the protective end of the spectrum, so I wasn't given as much freedom as some of my friends – surely Annie, at twenty-six, would have felt safe to do the same. To chat to a man in a pub she knew well, drink with him. Maybe even get in a car with him, if they'd been having a nice time.

It's an almost old-fashioned idea now, the woman who gets abducted because she walks home alone, or takes a lift from the wrong person. As children, we were aware not to get into a car with a stranger, although the definition of a stranger is pliable in rural areas where perhaps you know someone to see, but not to talk to. Anyway, knowing it's not safe doesn't matter – there's often no other way to get home. Even nowadays, public transport is scarce in Ireland, with one bus an hour serving most villages and perhaps a long walk to the stop. There are only a few main train lines, and even when you arrive at Dublin airport it's not unusual to wait an hour for a coach going north, only to find it's full and you have to wait another hour for the next. In many rural areas, taxis are hard to find and need to be pre-booked. As of 2019, Ireland only spends 0.6 per cent of its tax revenue on public transport. So what are the options? You walk. Or maybe you get into a car with someone, although some of the available drivers may be drunk. Drink-driving rates are still very high in the Irish countryside, sometimes simply because there is no alternative – a recent survey found that one in ten people had done it within the last year, and this would have been even more common in the nineties. If Annie wanted to go out for the day, and stay late for a drink, she would have needed to walk, or take a lift, or both. Perhaps because of this lack of transport in Ireland, if you see someone you know even slightly out and about without a car, it's common practice to offer them a lift, and for them to accept. Certainly in the eighties and nineties, when we still thought that non-sectarian murders didn't really happen, it was completely normal.

This also makes me think of the Wests, cruising the bus stops of Cheltenham for girls to pick up and murder, girls who wouldn't feel scared to see a man in the car with his wife, or the way the Moors murderers did the same. Did something like that happen in these cases? As we've already seen, two of the women murdered before the nineties were last seen waiting at bus stops, on almost the same date twelve years apart. They had both been Christmas shopping and might have been loaded down with bags. Maybe they'd have welcomed a lift, especially from someone they knew slightly (it would turn out that one did know her killer a little).

Once I noticed this aspect of Annie's disappearance – that she had been travelling about the countryside alone – I saw parallels with another of the cases. In 1995, on a cold dark November night, another young woman would go missing in the vanishing triangle, never to be seen again. This time she would die – because surely she is dead – because she missed a bus, rather than because she caught one. Jo Jo Dullard was twenty-one, the youngest of a close family whose mother had died when she was young. Her father had died before she was born. Her sisters, Kathleen and Mary, had brought her up as somewhere between an aunt and a sibling to their own children. Jo Jo had been working in Dublin, trying to become a beautician, but found it too expensive, and decided she didn't like to be so far from home, so she moved back to Kilkenny. That day, Jo Jo had gone up to Dublin to collect a dole payment and see some friends. She stayed late drinking in a bar called Bruxelles and missed the last bus home. As I've said, her options would have been very limited at this point. Without much money, she could do nothing but take a bus as far as she could, deep into the Irish countryside, then hitch the remaining miles back home. It was the middle of the night already, and she was a lone woman, slight and looking even younger than her age. She must have been afraid, or at least daunted by the long, cold journey ahead of her. But she must also have felt she had no other choice.

When I was in my teens I never hitch-hiked, but I knew people who did, and I definitely got lifts from people I didn't know all that well. When we started driving, I had friends, young female friends, who picked up hitch-hikers. A car is everything in the countryside. It's freedom. It's safety. It's power. That night, Jo Jo got a bus as far as she could, to the town of Naas, but she still had forty miles to travel. She was wearing jeans and boots, a zip-up jacket that can't have been warm enough in November. We know she safely hitched part of the way home because she used a phone box in a small village called Moone to ring her friend Mary, telling her what had happened and explaining that she was waiting for a lift. If not for this phone call, it's possible her family wouldn't even have known where she disappeared, whether she had been taken in Dublin or somewhere along the way. The search area would have been enormous. The phone box logged her call at 11.37 p.m. While talking to her friend, Jo Jo abruptly broke off, then hurriedly returned, saying she had a lift. That was the last time anyone saw or heard from her. She didn't show up for her job in a pub the next day, a Friday. That was when her family knew she was missing – but all the same it took three days to interest the Gardaí in her case. Certainly no one started looking for her until the Monday.

Once they got going, Gardaí did search extensively, interviewing over 800 people. They even called in a clairvoyant, something that's not unusual in Ireland. Gradually, they built a picture of her movements that night, the lifts she had taken. People said they'd seen a woman hitching in Castledermot, which is five miles on from Moone where she made the call. If this was Jo Jo, she might have got the lift from the phone box safely, but still not made it home, getting out again only to be picked up by someone else. Four different people reported a sighting in Castledermot, but no one ever came forward to say they'd driven her that far. A woman rang in anonymously to say she'd been in a car with Jo Jo and two men that night, but got out in Carlow, leaving Jo Jo with them (Carlow is where Larry Murphy attacked the woman in 2000, the one who narrowly survived, whose case was at the start of the book). Then, some time later, a taxi driver came forward to say that he'd seen something the night Jo Jo went missing – a woman in bare feet, trying to run from a car while a man peed near it, and being pulled back into it by the hair. He thought there were two men with the girl. It took him over a year to report it. This sighting was also over fifty miles away from Moone, near the city of Waterford, and was at almost one thirty in the morning. Waterford, by the way, was where another woman had gone missing the year before, in 1994. There was another tip-off even later, in 1999, from a couple who said they'd seen a woman and two men that night, the woman seemingly in a bad way, as if she were drunk or injured, walking in a forest. This was not far from the possible Waterford sighting, and the area was searched but nothing found.

You have to wonder why these possible witnesses didn't intervene, or if they somehow weren't able to, if it's the kind of thing you just drive past and you've already gone by the time your brain reminds you that wasn't normal. Or if it's some kind of bystander effect, where you might hear screams or see something strange, but assume that if it's important someone else will report it. It's difficult to be accurate about dates and times even days after an incident, so after months or years it's hardly likely to be helpful. It's another element that seems to recur throughout these stories – people see something suspicious, but they don't do anything about it. They don't call the police. They keep silent.

A number of suspects emerged from the initial enquiry: two cousins, members of the travelling community, who were known to have abducted and raped at least one woman, but that lead petered out. There were two Englishmen in the area around that time, stealing money from phone boxes – and Jo Jo had been in a phone box when she made that last call. The car the woman had allegedly tried to run from near Waterford was reported to have had English plates, so that could have been a possible lead – but these thieving men were tracked down and traced to Cork, on the other side of the country, and they had an alibi for the whole night. As always, none of it came to anything. Jo Jo's family did their best. They even hired a private investigator to go on to the farmland of someone they suspected, a few months after she went missing. This man had scratches on his face, the investigator said, as if someone had fought him – Jo Jo was known to keep her nails long. I've also been told, though admittedly second hand, that this man once got Jo Jo's sister against a wall, weeping and saying he was sorry for what he'd done. But, as in so many of these cases, the evidence is circumstantial, easily explained away, with no proof, and so nothing can come of it.

The search for Jo Jo devastated her family, as they agonised over what to do and what might have happened to her. Were the police doing enough? Was that man's land ever searched? It seems not. Although searches were carried out in other places, and the army even called in to help, was this just a PR exercise while the chief suspect was ignored? I don't know who this suspect was – everything is discussed so carefully in the press, and so much of it is nothing more than rumour. False hope, baseless sightings, crank claims:

they came and went. The family were even harassed by a man who said Jo Jo had been involved in a satanic cult.

In 1997 a body was found miles away in the River Shannon, badly decomposed. It took weeks to confirm that this was not Jo Jo; in fact, it was a man's body. But her family had to find out by hearing the announcement on the radio like everyone else, since the Gardaí had not told them before the news was made public. I wonder what it must be like, to know a body has been found, and perhaps partly hope that it is your sister or your daughter, because then at least you'd know, but also to hope that it isn't, because then she might possibly, just possibly, still be alive.

I had known about Annie and Jo Jo's cases before, though not in much detail. However, I was surprised to learn that yet another woman had been murdered in the vanishing triangle during this time – Marilyn Rynn, who disappeared just a month after Jo Jo in 1995. This time, however, her body was found, and a man convicted of her murder. Like so many of these women, Marilyn, who had just turned forty-one, was attacked around Christmas, in the early hours of 22 December. Another Christmas disappearance: I wonder if there's a pattern, or if it's just that people go out more around then, they drink more, and maybe they let their guard down. Marilyn, who had a good job in the Department of the Environment, was out at a work Christmas do that night, on the outskirts of Dublin. Afterwards, she went into the city to meet a friend and get some food. Then, instead of taking a taxi to where she lived on the Northside – which, a news report from the time tells me, *she had the money to do*, as if she shares some blame for being raped and murdered – she chose to take the bus then walk the short route home through a park. There would likely have been an hour-long wait for cabs, so I can understand why she did this. The path she chose was dangerous, and several robberies had happened there, but it was already almost 4 a.m. and to go round the park would have taken half an hour instead of just a few minutes. It was a calculated risk.

As it was, Marilyn would be one of the unlucky ones. While she was walking down the dark path, she passed the man who would murder her. Before this, he'd never done anything out of the ordinary, or not that we know of. He earned good money as a telecoms engineer, was married with a young child. That night he'd been drinking steadily, also out at his work Christmas do, and as he passed Marilyn, some notion took him, something made him pull her into the bushes, rape and strangle her, and leave her naked body discarded there. Once he had raped and killed her, this man went home and got into bed beside his wife, who never suspected a thing, just as Larry Murphy would do the night he raped and almost killed a woman in Carlow. He took his child to school in the morning, went to work. Carried on with his life. It seems incredible, but, interviewed on a *Crimeline* documentary about it, detective Alan Bailey said, 'They never show it, these men.' I found that terrifying, the idea that such violent murder leaves no trace. He did, however, put his clothes in the wash, in the middle of the night, which is suspicious enough in itself. I wonder what his wife thought, if she noticed.

Marilyn's family started to worry when she didn't turn up for Christmas dinner a few days later. Even though she was killed very close to her home, her body was not found until 6 January, which must have made for an unendurable few weeks for her family, her parents and brother and sister, nieces and nephews. Questions were asked about why she wasn't found for so long, when her route home would have been obvious, and she wasn't buried or hidden. It makes you wonder, if it took two weeks to find her, how hard they have looked for women whose bodies were most likely actually hidden, who have never been found. Admittedly, part of the reason for this delay was that a friend had called the Gardaí, adamant that she'd spoken to Marilyn the day *after* the Christmas do, which was the 22nd, and that they'd arranged to go shopping. This made police think she had got home safe from her work party, and disappeared sometime after that. It later turned out the friend had the day wrong, and they'd actually spoken on the 21st. It just goes to show how unreliable memories are even a few days after an event, let alone twenty years later.

In one of those 'Ireland is small' coincidences, detectives found that a man who'd known Marilyn had also known Annie McCarrick. Hackles went up. Was this the connection that had eluded Gardaí, something linking all these dead and missing women? That's all it was though – a coincidence. Marilyn's killer was caught not long after, a man named David Lawler. But it's further proof that someone out there must know more than they've said. You can't hide things in a country this size. Not unless people keep quiet. Which we have a lot of practice of, in Ireland.

So in late 1995, we have a suspect emerging in the triangle area, a man who was capable of rape and murder. Had David Lawler done it before? He was thirty-one at the time, so could have been in the picture for the earlier disappearances and even the murders, the women buried in the mountains. Yet again, however, there was nothing to link him to any of them, and he was convicted of Marilyn's murder alone. He was caught because he had left DNA evidence all over her body, perhaps thinking it could not survive for long outdoors, and so he cooperated when the Gardaí sampled men in the area. As in one of the earlier murders, however, the cold temperatures preserved the DNA, and Lawler became the first person in Ireland to be convicted this way. Gardaí could see that he had searched the internet for information about DNA and how long it remains viable. The case must also be one of the first where computer technology was used to help convict. If not for those two factors – DNA and technology – I wonder if he might still be free today. Given the MO, the fact he didn't try to hide the body at all, it seems unlikely Lawler was involved in the other cases. There's another side to it, of course: if he had nothing to do with them, and Marilyn was his only victim, then just how many sexual predators were there in Ireland at this time?

Annie McCarrick caught her bus on the day she vanished, and went for a walk by herself, which must have seemed a low-risk decision. Jo Jo missed hers, and had to hitch. I wonder how her friend Mary feels, if she wishes she could call Jo Jo back at the phone box, tell her not to get into that car. But wouldn't a warm car seem better than a phone box at the side of the road, in the middle of a November night? Jo Jo had taken several other lifts that night, and all had been fine – she must have thought it a small risk. Likewise, Marilyn decided for whatever reason to walk the short distance home, and she died. That these tiny decisions, these split-second differences, can alter the course of our lives, is tough to accept.

These cases – Annie, Jo Jo, Marilyn – seem like classic, tragic, cautionary tales. Women travelling alone around country lanes, walking through parks at night, hitching lifts with strangers. Ending up missing or dead. But if we judge them for their choices, what are we saying – it was their fault? It's easy to say they should have taken taxis, regardless of the expense, or they should have gone home earlier or they shouldn't have been out in the first place. Even in London, where I live, and transport is (just about) available late at night, women are still blamed if they run into danger while returning home. A famously victim-blaming campaign several years ago urged women to use black cabs – not minicabs or Ubers – to get home, or risk rape. Even if transport doesn't exist, or costs too much to use, it's still our responsibility somehow not to get attacked. But is that really the best we can offer as protection against a total stranger pulling you off the street, raping and murdering you, leaving your naked body behind to freeze and rot on waste ground, and be found days later, or not at all? Is there no onus on these men, you know, not to do it?

I've always been slightly baffled by the ways women are instructed to keep themselves safe. Get a taxi. Text me when you get in. Get a taxi, as if they don't cost a fortune (£60 in a black cab from the centre of town to where I live in London, and we're always being told how unsafe Uber is). Text me, as if your friend would stay awake till you got home and do something if you didn't check in (I usually forget anyway). As if the driver might not attack you anyway, like John Worboys, the so-called 'black cab rapist'. There are several cases of Irish men during this time posing as taxi drivers, picking up women only to drive them out to the mountains and assault them, and we know that one of the earlier murdered women was last seen sharing a taxi with two men. Sharing a cab with strangers was quite common in Ireland at this time, as a way to cut the cost, and again as a result of poor public transport links. So taxis aren't necessarily safe, and anyway it's dark by half three in the afternoon in winter; are we supposed to be home by then? There was also a case in 1994 where a girl was most likely murdered by the family friend who drove her to a disco, and just as I was finishing this book, a man in the UK was convicted of raping and killing the female friend he had walked home from her own birthday party. So if you can't take a taxi, or a trusted lift, or a random lift, or walk, what can you do?

For women trying to be independent – and all three were single – it means going out in the world. It means sometimes being out after dark, where things rustle in the bushes. It means taking a short cut to save yourself a half-hour walk. We can say that poor public transport probably contributed to several of these cases, that perhaps certain predators took advantage of that, and cruised the roads looking for women walking alone. We can perhaps even say that self-policing, being more careful, might help with this, but ultimately it's down to these men not to attack us. There must be better ways to keep women safe than by imposing a virtual curfew, or a tax, via expensive trips home, on not getting raped and murdered.

In 1996, a few months after Jo Jo disappeared, the first reference to a triangle appeared in the media, in an interview given by Annie McCarrick's father, John. Although he lived in New York, he was aware that Jo Jo had gone missing not far from the last sightings of Annie, as well as another woman later in 1993. He was perhaps not aware that yet another woman had also gone missing in 1994 in the same area, but he was linking the cases even then. So why did the Gardaí not start putting these cases together for several more years?

Chapter Three

INSTITUTIONS

It was becoming obvious that there were a lot of cases I needed to include in a study of those years, 1993 to 1998. As the names stacked up of women who were either dead or missing, I became more and more disturbed by the failure of the police to solve most of these cases or even to link them. By the end of the decade, the only case solved of all these murders and disappearances would be Marilyn Rynn's. I began to wonder if the fault lay at an institutional level. In the nineties, of course, Irish people were slowly becoming aware that the organisations they trusted and held dear, like the police, the state and most of all the Catholic Church, were often indifferent to individual suffering. By the start of the decade, we knew that priests in Ireland had been systematically abusing children for years, and that the Church, fully aware of this, had simply moved them around, allowing them access to even more victims. The story about Father Brendan Smyth, one of the most notorious abusers, broke in 1991, but he didn't go to jail until 1994, because, as we've seen, he simply went over the border and was protected there, even as the RUC tried to issue extradition warrants.

I was aware of the paedophile priests scandal, of course, even though I was only ten when it first hit the news. My granny and great-aunt, the one with the true crime books, both daily mass-goers, were shocked by it, and struggled to reconcile it with how heavily they leaned on the Church. So it wasn't a surprise to me to find out more about what the Church had done. But this was: realising that the IRA had done exactly the same thing, and also protected sexual predators. As a Northern Irish Catholic, I had grown up believing that the RUC, the Northern Irish police, was deeply flawed and biased. It's fair to say that, where I grew up in South Down, there was sympathy and even strong support for the IRA. There still is today. Even if people disapproved of their methods – and Catholics often died in their bombs too – most understood the basis of the cause. In some parts of Ireland, the IRA was seen as an alternative police force, and you could call them if your house was burgled or joy-riders took your car. All through the nineties it was common for the IRA to give 'punishment beatings' – usually breaking the knees with a baseball bat – for offences such as dealing drugs or stealing cars. But I didn't know that the IRA had covered up for men in their ranks who hurt children and women. I found this out while looking into Annie McCarrick's case.

As I mentioned, the night that the woman who might have been Annie McCarrick went to Johnnie Fox's pub, she was in the company of a man who was described as something of a yuppie. Later, though, it was alleged that this man was in fact an IRA member, who'd been sent south of the border after assaulting the daughter of another member of that organisation. That girl was twelve at the time, but the IRA took care of its own, in both senses of the phrase, and so just like the priests, the man was simply moved on instead of being handed over to police. I would not associate the word yuppie with an IRA member, but I suppose a terrorist could easily wear a waxed jacket, if that's all it meant.

To be honest, it hadn't occurred to me that there could be paramilitary involvement in any of these disappearances because they took place in Southern Ireland. In that way, I suppose I'm guilty of doing what I've accused others of, and pretending the border isn't totally porous or that you couldn't drive from Dublin to Belfast in just a few hours. It makes sense, actually. If an IRA man was involved, people with information would have been too scared to speak out. And the IRA knew how to hide bodies, some of which have never been found to this day. There is also precedent for this kind of thing happening in Republican circles, men being quietly moved on after committing crimes – after all, the organisation liked to dispense its own justice, often by way of knee-capping or a bullet in the head. Going to the police, or what were seen as unfair, British-imposed courts, many of them run without juries during the Troubles, would not have been an option. In some cases, though, it appears they just moved the men away and did nothing to stop them.

Gerry Adams is perhaps the most significant figure in all of Irish Republicanism. Several years ago, his niece said she was abused as a child by her father, Adams's brother, between the ages of four and ten. He was convicted of the abuse in 2013. She also said that her Uncle Gerry had known about this since 1987, and he admitted he had (although he said this was only after it stopped, and that the police had known too since the early nineties). His brother had actually confessed to him in 2000, but it appears he didn't tell the police this, or do anything about it, even when his brother started working at a youth club. Aine, who waived her right to anonymity in court, has said that her uncle tried to pressure her into not going public, and even to obtain a court injunction so the story would not come out in the press. In 2015, several people came forward and said they'd been raped by another IRA member, and not only had they been stopped from going to the police, but they were also threatened to make them keep their silence. One was the niece of another prominent IRA man, Joe Cahill. These men were clearly willing to put the Republican cause before their own families. The victims claimed the man who abused them was quietly moved to England. It's very hard to be sure since none of these men are named, but I think this must be a different person to the man allegedly with Annie McCarrick in the pub, as he's reported to be living in Texas now.

These cases show how the IRA functioned to shield men like this. How politics trumped other crimes, like rape, like child abuse. How Ireland was so ruled by ideology at the time that women and children were being crushed in the middle. In 2010, Gardaí were told that the supposed IRA man had admitted to giving Annie a lift that night. IRA suspects in the South were at the time not extradited back to the North across the non-existent border, perhaps another case of the island's dark history coiling around these cases. He said he'd dropped Annie off at a bus stop, safe and sound, but there was speculation: what if he'd started boasting about his past, trying to impress this beautiful young American girl, who so wanted to know the 'real' Ireland? What if he told her too much, revealed operational secrets? Like every lead, however, it ultimately came to nothing.

It wasn't just the Church and the IRA that protected dangerous men. In some ways, the state itself, and the criminal justice system, did too. In many of the cases in this book, when a man is finally caught for killing or hurting a woman, he's found to have committed violent crimes before. Often he will have served time, only to be let out so quickly it's shocking, and reoffend. Here's one example. In 2001 in Drogheda, a town not far from the border, another young German tourist, Bettina Poeschel, was savagely murdered. Bettina, who was twenty-eight and a journalist on the last day of a week-long visit to Ireland, was walking along a road in the countryside in the middle of the day, on her way to Newgrange, a prehistoric burial site that's a popular tourist attraction. Once a year, on the winter solstice, the light hits the chamber at just the right angle to fill it. Bettina, like Jo Jo Dullard, had missed a bus, but it was the middle of the day so she must have felt safe to walk. She wasn't. A man was working on the road in motorway construction, and he saw her go past and decided to go after her. Her body was found three weeks later hidden in undergrowth. She'd been raped, and her underwear had traces of disinfectant on it, which the man had taken from his work. Presumably he was trying, very ineptly, to erase his DNA. Her killer, nicknamed 'the Monster', was called Michael Murphy (no relation to Larry), and he had done this many times before, including strangling an elderly woman to death in the eighties, and assaulting several other women in 1997. Yet he served just eight years for that murder, and six months for the sexual assaults – he got longer for some robberies he'd also committed. Could he have carried out other murders and assaults that the police just didn't know about? He claimed he had been overcome by an uncontrollable urge to take Bettina as she walked along the road – in broad daylight, at 11.30 a.m., near a major tourist attraction – and strangle her. If he hadn't been allowed out so soon after his last murder, or if he'd been monitored more carefully, perhaps Bettina would still be alive. Drogheda falls into the vanishing triangle as well, so here's yet another sexual predator operating in that area in the nineties. Once again, however, Gardaí weren't able to link him to any other cases.

Here's another case. In 1999 a man called Philip Colgan picked up a woman named Layla Brennan (no relation to Eva, one of the women who went missing in 1993) in his car, drove her out to the Wicklow Mountains – right in the middle of the vanishing triangle – and murdered her. Layla was known to have been a drug addict and had done sex work in the past. Colgan was not long out of prison for raping two other women in quick succession, one of whom was seventy-nine years old. Both of these attacks took place in late 1991, and yet he was out of prison by 1999. Eight years, for raping two women. In prison, he fell for one of the female staff, who married him as soon as he was released. Layla was taken from Dublin, strangled with her own bra, supposedly after a row about payment for sex work, and her body hidden in the Wicklow Mountains. Colgan immediately confessed to his wife what he'd done – she had married him knowing he had two convictions for rape, of course – and she made him go to the police, so Layla's body was at least found. Committing two rapes so close together is a sign of escalation, loss of control, and yet he was allowed out again, and just months later he had murdered a woman.

Colgan was out of the picture for the triangle disappearances, but I include this case to show how dangerous it is not to heed the warning signs when men hurt women. Almost always they will go on to do it again, and worse. And lessons have not been learned from any of this. Larry Murphy, the Carlow rapist, got out of prison in 2010 after just nine years. As he committed his crime before the Sex Offenders Act came into force in Ireland, he's not officially monitored at all, and has since lived in Amsterdam, Spain and also apparently south London, where I live now. He's only in his fifties.

I want to talk now about a case that doesn't fall into the vanishing triangle area, but which I think could easily be linked. It's a case that illustrates the total failure of the justice system to protect young women. This woman was just a girl really, fifteen years old. Arlene Arkinson lived in Northern Ireland, and the chief suspect in her case was known to move around a lot between different parts of Ireland and the UK. He had to, because everywhere he went he would hurt a woman, usually a young girl. Arlene disappeared only a few hours from Dublin, and at the time no physical border existed between North and South, a life-saving fudge that the EU made possible. In fact, Arlene had crossed into the South for a night out, but she never made it home. The border is perhaps one reason her case has been overlooked. Another reason, maybe, is that it's always been clear what happened to her.

I don't remember hearing about Arlene's disappearance. All I remember from this year, 1994, is the endless onslaught of political news, as IRA ceasefires were made, sustained, then fell apart. I remember holding my breath for a year – let it be over. Please, let it be over. Easy for a missing girl to be overlooked, in all that fate-of-a-nation rhetoric. But shouldn't someone have told us? If a teenage girl had been murdered, shouldn't they have warned the rest of us? The start of Arlene's story is achingly familiar to me. She had crossed the border from where she lived in Castlederg, County Tyrone, to go to a disco in Bundoran, Donegal. I used to go to country discos too, in hotels or parish halls, under-age discos with a mineral bar and no alcohol, a fug of smoke and hairspray and cheap aftershave, where even at that age you couldn't cross the dancefloor without being groped by some farmer's son from the next village over. Sometimes I even went over the border to go to them. Bundoran, where Arlene went that night, is a place I know well from teenage trips to the Gaeltacht, the Irish-speaking part of Ireland. When I thought about this, I realised I had actually been at the Gaeltacht in August 1994. I was twelve, my first time away from home and I would have been staying just over an hour away from Bundoran, in the village of Dun Luiche. We even went to Bundoran once or twice for the evening.

All the same, I don't remember hearing Arlene's name. Arlene was getting a lift with her friend and friend's boyfriend, driven by the new partner of her friend's mother. The man who drove Arlene to the disco that night and, according to him, dropped her safely back outside her house, would later murder another teenage girl in England. Yet he was ruled out of the investigation into Arlene's disappearance, and wasn't put on trial for her murder until 2005, by which time he was already in prison for murdering the other young girl. And because of Northern Irish court rules, which wouldn't have applied in England and Wales, the jury in Arlene's case weren't allowed to know about his other conviction, and so he was acquitted. The new boyfriend's name was Robert Howard – Robert 'the Wolfman' Howard.

In her pictures, Arlene is smiling. Her eyes are a striking blue. She loved art, her sister said. She was the youngest sibling of seven children, whose mother had died when she was eleven, whose father struggled with drink, who was raised by her sisters. That makes sense too – men like Robert Howard, who are known to target young girls, often go for more vulnerable ones, where there might be less outcry when they vanish. Arlene wanted to move to England; she had talked about running away, one of her friends said. There are many baffling things about this case. For example, the fact that she was last seen in the car of a man who'd previously served ten years in prison for rape; who had, when younger, tried to rape a six-year-old child; who nonetheless was believed when he said he'd dropped Arlene safely home. The fact that, instead of charging him, the RUC went round to the house of Arlene's sister, Kathleen, who had four young children herself, and knocked her door in with a sledgehammer, put her in handcuffs and arrested her partner, then brought in JCB diggers to rip up her garden. Kathleen has since launched a civil suit against the police for their actions.

The year before Arlene disappeared, a sixteen-year-old girl had gone to the RUC and said she'd just escaped from Robert Howard's flat, where he'd held her for several days and raped her, putting a rope around her neck to stop her getting away. The police seemed to hardly believe her, so apathetic was their response, even though they searched his flat and found a rope just as she said. He was charged with rape but allowed out on bail; the charge was later downgraded to sexual assault and he was given a suspended sentence, with no time served. It was while he was on bail from that offence that he drove Arlene and her friends to the disco, and Arlene never came home.

I find this so hard to believe, even knowing what I do about the RUC at this time, even knowing what else happened that year, the bombs and shootings and wobbling peace process. It still shocks me, and maybe that's good – we should be shocked by how this keeps happening, older and powerful men being listened to and the girls and women they hurt not being believed. Another thing that shocked me was to read that Robert Howard had lived in Newry for a while in the nineties – that's the nearest town to where I grew up; I went to secondary school there. Again, I don't recall hearing a word about the case or about this man who might have been driving around, looking for girls. All this seems to make no sense. I then stumbled on an article that might have explained why the case was handled so strangely – Robert Howard was rumoured to be a police informant.

If I were inventing this case for one of my books, that's exactly the kind of dramatic explanation I would put in for all these bizarre failures – the obvious suspect was not arrested because he had political connections. But if this sounds far-fetched, something you'd only find in a novel, remember that anything was possible in Northern Ireland during the Troubles. A senior member of the IRA punishment squad in the eighties and nineties, who was responsible for rooting out and killing informers, has for a long time been alleged to have also been 'Stakeknife', a high-level informant for the RUC and Army within the IRA. To safeguard its source, it's been suggested, the British Army allowed several innocent people to be killed, both by this man and one time instead of him, in a case of mistaken identity. So it's not totally unbelievable that the police would allow a man who'd killed a teenage girl to go free if he was useful to them, if he was perhaps feeding them information of some kind. Certainly an inquest into Arlene's death was told this, in 2016, and some of the documents relating to the case were held under Public Interest Immunity, which more commonly relates to terror or national security matters, not what we might call 'ordinary' murders.

To be fair to what is now the PSNI, they have looked for Arlene. They're still looking – in 2018 there were new excavations in the search for her, though they didn't find anything. All the same, they let Howard go free back in 1994, took his word for what had happened, even though it makes no sense that he'd drop his girlfriend's daughter off first, then drive her friend away, just the two of them alone, only then to come back to the first house. Kathleen Arkinson, Arlene's sister, talking about the bewildering decision of the RUC to break down her door rather than arresting the obvious suspect, said that if Howard got away with it, someone else would die. She was right about that. In April 2001, in Dartford, Kent, another girl went missing. Hannah Williams was fourteen, a working-class girl who had run away before, and it would be almost a year before she was found dead. Her decomposing body was found by workers on the Channel Tunnel in 2002. She had a rope wrapped around her neck when she was found. Robert Howard was arrested for Hannah's murder the next day, and this time he was convicted.

The Gardaí think Howard might have hurt many other women and children during the eight years he was free after Arlene disappeared – he's been looked at for up to fifteen unsolved murders in Ireland and the UK. Even when he eventually went on trial for Arlene's murder, as we've seen, he was acquitted. So although everyone knows what probably happened to Arlene, he got off, meaning no justice for her family. Meaning no closure. Meaning he didn't have to say where he'd put her. Still no body, no grave to visit. No answers. He died in prison in 2015, of a heart attack, without ever saying a word. Arlene was failed by the law, by the RUC and by the simple fact of living near a border.

There was also the fact that fear of terrorists saturated every aspect of life at this time. For example, two years after Arlene went missing, in 1996, a burial was taking place at a country churchyard not far from where she lived, when something else was uncovered. A body was already there in the ground, not in a coffin. This being Ireland, and the peace process so fragile, the gravediggers and priest simply never told anyone. Privately, they thought it could have been the body of Arlene Arkinson. But they didn't do anything. I find that astonishing, like so many of the facts in this story. Years later – in 2018 – this body would finally be exhumed, and it wasn't Arlene. But someone must have been missing them all that time, over twenty years. It tells you a lot about Ireland in the mid-nineties, how weak the peace was, and how thoroughly people had been schooled not to talk about what they knew. Even when it was a matter of a dead teenage girl. Even a priest, a pillar of the community, had been silenced by the culture, the fear. People would rather a family suffered in agony than risk speaking out. The Church let Arlene down too.

I was not much younger than Arlene Arkinson when she went missing – in summer 1994 I was twelve. Despite my age, I would not have been terribly surprised to learn that the state, the Church and, yes, even the terrorist organisations who claimed to fight for my community and my freedom, would have thrown me under a bus in a heartbeat. That, if I were murdered, the police might bungle the case so badly my killer would walk free. I had, after all, been aware of the Child X case that had torn Ireland apart a couple of years before, in 1992. A fourteen-year-old girl had been raped by a neighbour, and since there was no abortion in Ireland and wouldn't be for almost thirty more years, her family took her to England to get one. When the state learned about this – the family had asked if the Gardaí would need the DNA evidence from the foetus in order to prosecute the rapist – it invoked the constitution, forced her to return home, and took away the family's passports. On appeal, this judgement was struck down, but by then the girl had had a miscarriage. The man who raped her served just three years in prison. As early as 1999, he was once again convicted of assaulting an underage girl, and went back to prison. He served another three years and out he came, his sentence reduced from fourteen years because, the judge said, he was a 'hard-working family man'. I find it striking that in the reports of the case, people don't want to use the word rape, even when legally that's what it is, whether the girl thought so at the time or not.

Child C was a similar case, in 1997: she was thirteen and had also been raped by an older man. In this case, her parents, who were from the travelling community and pro-lifers, didn't want her to have an abortion, but because of the earlier ruling on Child X, she was allowed to be taken to England for the procedure, her own decision. It seems completely insane that such matters – allowing a girl barely into puberty not to have her rapist's baby – were being debated at the highest level of government, and that in the Child X case, the state felt it could put someone under virtual house arrest to stop them leaving the country, but that was Ireland in the nineties. In the C case, her rapist was imprisoned but also struck again once he was released, attacking a woman in her eighties. He's still in prison now for that crime. It's astonishing how often these men do it again, and again, and again, and only stop when they're locked up.

As part of my research, I spoke to Fay Maxted, CEO of the Survivors Trust, an organisation supporting rape crisis centres in

Ireland and the UK. She mentioned the poor treatment of rape survivors by the police and courts, and the slow follow-up of cases due to cuts in the police and legal services – though we're not as bad as America, where thousands of rape kits have sat untested for decades due to backlogs in the system, lack of funding, lack of will. Imagine knowing your rapist was out there in the world, not because the conviction fell through, but because no one had even bothered to look at the evidence yet. Such lack of urgency sends a clear message to victims – you don't matter. And even more so when your rapist is released after just a few years and does it again. Fay says lessons also need to be learned about offender management, to stop letting these men disappear and start a new life, or have their records expunged as if nothing ever happened.

I've always been a liberal and can see the damage long, punitive prison sentences do, especially when the initial crime was minor, like those serving decades in America for possessing weed, which is now legal in many states. Yet it strikes me that so many of these women and girls would be alive now if someone had paid heed the first time a man revealed his true self. In cases like Robert Howard's, he was only a child himself when he committed his first crime, and twenty when he first assaulted someone, the start of a pattern of rape and eventually murder that went on for over forty years. It's also true that Ireland doesn't have the best record when it comes to rape conviction rates. Of all the rape cases tried in the country leading up to 1993, only three had ever resulted in sentences of more than seven years, and many were suspended, so the rapists served no time at all. Between 1998 and 2001, the rape conviction rate in the country was just 1 per cent, the lowest in Europe, and two prominent cases in 2018 would demonstrate that this culture is sadly alive and well. A 2002 survey suggested that almost a third of Irish women had been abused as children – this is clearly a country with a widespread problem of sexual violence. Repeatedly, the suspects and murderers in these cases were found to have committed previous crimes. They didn't commit murder out of the blue. There was almost always a trail of rapes, of assaults, even of attempted murders behind them, and yet they were still free to repeat their crimes.

An acquaintance who's a police officer, who used to work in a Sapphire unit, one that deals with sexual offences, once told me wearily that her job there had included checking up on men who were out of prison after committing rapes or the sexual abuse of children. There was no rehabilitation, she said. Officers were always just waiting for it to happen again, and hoping they could catch the men in time. So perhaps part of the reason so many women went missing in the nineties is that violent men are sheltered, treated with leniency, or their cases bungled so they weren't convicted despite obvious guilt.

In this chapter are several more examples of killers in Ireland, men who raped and murdered, including Robert Howard, who was roaming about the country in the nineties. If I were writing this story in one of my novels, the police would be able to prove that one of those men killed the triangle women, and the cases would be solved. Sadly, in real life, it wasn't that simple. Instead of finding one obvious red-flag suspect, I was finding several. It was starting to feel as if the violent murder, as well as the rape, of women in Ireland was not as unusual as I'd thought.

Chapter Four

INDIFFERENCE

During my research, certain names loomed very large, while others I had to dig for. Annie McCarrick's 1993 case – a beautiful young American girl in love with Ireland – at least got attention. There was a full-scale hunt for her, with FBI agents even visiting from America. But later that same year, in July, another woman would go missing and barely receive a second thought. Eva Brennan was thirty-nine when she left her family's home in Rathgar, Dublin, to walk back to her own place. Rathgar is ten miles from Enniskerry, where Annie McCarrick likely disappeared just a few months before. There was a minor family row – Eva didn't want to have lamb again for Sunday lunch and was annoyed when she saw it cooking in the oven. One of her brothers had said she could leave if she didn't like it, I imagine jokingly, and she had gone off, as my family would say, in a 'huff'. She had short brown hair, and was wearing a pink tracksuit and a man's watch, carrying a red bag. Eva typically saw her parents every day. Two days later, when she still hadn't come over, her worried father went to her flat and broke in. He had persuaded her not to buy a ground-floor one, concerned for her safety. Had something happened to her anyway?

At the flat, he found the jacket she'd worn on the Sunday. So she had at least made it home after the row, and then perhaps gone out again, maybe for a walk as it was a nice day. But where was she now? Eva was close to her parents, who owned two pubs in the area, and to her six siblings, who felt the police simply did nothing. As far as the family know, they didn't even fingerprint Eva's flat for three months. They seemed to decide she had killed herself – she was known to have been depressed in the past – and that was that, despite the family's insistence that she would not have done such a thing. Eva was a very religious person, who was extremely involved with her family and wouldn't have wanted to cause them pain. Her social life revolved around the Church and her prayer group. For both these reasons, her family insist, she would never have killed herself, and yet that's what the police concluded, why they didn't look for her until it was perhaps too late. She wasn't included in the case review that Operation Trace carried out at the end of the decade, maybe because the Gardaí were so sure it was suicide, or maybe because she was older than the other women (though she looked young; and would someone really have been able to tell her age just at a glance, say if they saw her walking along a road as they were driving past?). Marilyn Rynn was murdered and raped by a stranger, and she was two years older than Eva. Many of the suspects in these cases killed and raped a wide variety of women, from children to elderly ladies – they did not discriminate.

Unlike for Annie McCarrick, there is no CCTV footage of Eva Brennan. Barely any pictures, and scant information online about her case. In the only photo I can find of her, she wears a flowered shirt and looks away from the camera, touching her mouth as if anxious or pensive. In 2013, twenty years after her disappearance, her family put out another appeal – you can almost feel the weariness in their statement. *We want to bring the search to a conclusion*, it read. They know she must be dead, or else she would be back with them. She wouldn't have stayed away all these years. They just want to bury her.

Colette McCann, Eva's sister, was interviewed on the *Ray D'Arcy Show*, one of Irish radio's flagship programmes, a few years ago. She said that, back in 1993, she had suggested to Gardaí a serial killer might be at work in the area – they knew all about Annie McCarrick's case several months before, and Enniskerry, where Annie was last seen, was just half an hour's drive from Eva's flat. Despite this, Colette said she was 'pooh-poohed'. It doesn't happen here, the police said – as if they could not contemplate that sort of murder, a woman taken from her home or the side of a road by some brutal stranger. This was Ireland, not America. No, it must have been suicide. The police said this even though they must have been aware that Annie was probably killed by a stranger, and that several other women had been murdered in the same area in previous years. And, as Colette pointed out, even if Eva had killed herself, where was her body? She didn't bury herself, did she? Wouldn't she have been found by now if she had taken her own life? Colette said she took comfort in thinking of her father, who died in 2001, and Eva in heaven together, happy at last. Sadly, Colette herself died in 2016, without ever finding out what happened to her sister. That's all there is to know – the trail went cold. Eva hasn't been seen in twenty-seven years.

Why had I never heard Eva Brennan's name before? Why do some missing women get attention, posters everywhere, TV reconstructions, the FBI involved, and some get nothing? There is actually a term for this – *missing white girl phenomenon*. Not just race but class plays a role too. As we saw in the last chapter, the girl that Robert Howard killed in England, Hannah Williams, went missing in 2001, but even though I was living there at the time, I'd never heard her name before researching this book. Hannah was missing for almost a year before her body was found. I had, on the other hand, heard all about Milly Dowler, who went missing just a month later, not far away, and was found dead after nine months. This has also been cited as a factor in the Madeleine McCann case, a reason for the onslaught of publicity that ironically may have cast her parents in a guilty light, when in fact a child goes missing every two minutes in the EU. (While I was in the final stages of editing this book, new information has emerged linking Madeleine's disappearance to a serial sex offender living in the area, who seems to have been overlooked at the time, while the family were interrogated over and over.) The individual cases obscure and mask the real statistics, the fact that maybe people come to harm more often than we think. If I were her family, I would have been hurt and angry that Eva wasn't included in the cold-case review, that she was simply forgotten about because of her mental health history, and her age.

◆ ◆ ◆

Even after researching these cases for years, I kept finding new names, women dead or missing in the triangle who I'd never heard of before, who hadn't been linked to the other cases. Maybe because certain assumptions were made, such as suicide, as in Eva Brennan's case. Or because there was an obvious suspect. There are lots of examples. Marie Kilmartin, for instance. She was found dead that same year, 1993, and buried in the same mountains. She had been put into a bog drain, a concrete block weighing down her chest, along with a lot of other rubbish including a broken gas heater and a pram. Again, Marie went missing near Christmas – 16 December 1992 – and her body was found six months later, in County Laois where she lived (less than a hundred miles from Dublin). Marie, who was thirty-five and worked in a care home, is an example of someone who might have been dismissed by police. She was older than the women looked at by Operation Trace, all in their teens and twenties. She'd also had a child despite not being married, who had been adopted within the extended family. In what seems to me an unbearably sad twist, the girl – now grown up – attended Marie's funeral without being told that this was her mother. Like Eva Brennan, Marie was known to have been depressed in the past, and had spent time in institutions – did that mean her case wasn't given the priority it should have had?

Portlaoise is only an hour's drive from where two of the earlier murdered women were also found buried in the bog, and half an hour from Newbridge, where a woman went missing in 1979 and another in 1998. It's forty minutes from Carlow, where the brutal rape took place in 2000. Close enough to be connected, perhaps. Marie was last seen going into her house around four in the afternoon, and the Gardaí were able to show that someone rang her home from a phone box not long after. Did she go out to meet that person? When her flatmate got home that night at six, Marie wasn't there. She had set the house alarm, but not put away her shopping, which suggests that, as in Annie's case, she intended to be back soon. Gardaí felt two people might have been involved, to lift such heavy items into her grave with her. Her body was quite well hidden, found only by chance by someone cutting turf, because water levels had dropped in the area after a hot summer. However, once again, the trail went cold.

Now Marie's daughter Aoife has found out the truth about her mother, she has been fighting to get the case reopened. It was announced in 2008 that three people, two men and a woman, had been arrested, and when I looked into it recently, one chief suspect had been re-questioned, but so far no charges have been brought.

To me, these two cases, Eva's disappearance and Marie's murder, say a lot about how we deal with mental illness in Ireland. That we can't see there's a big leap between suffering from occasional depression and killing yourself over a small family row. That we write off women who are older, who don't have children or have them when they're not married, or who stay single; that perhaps we can't understand how a woman who's almost forty could be a victim of a sexual predator. Ireland has the fourth-highest rate of suicide in Europe among young people, and at least one person kills themselves every day. Northern Ireland currently has the highest suicide rate in the UK. In the nineties, mental health was rarely discussed and I had never heard of anyone seeing a counsellor or therapist in the course of normal life. The stigma around suicide was still huge, and within recent memory, people who took their own lives could not be buried in a Catholic graveyard. Suicide rates rose sharply in Ireland from the seventies, peaking in 1998, although it's much more common among men than women. It's also estimated that suicide was under-reported by as much as 40 per cent in the past, because of the stigma – it remained a criminal offence in Ireland until 1993 (as opposed to 1961 in England). Attitudes were softening in the 1990s, and I don't think the burial rule would have been enforced, but there was still a very real sense of shame. Perhaps these attitudes to mental health and suicide, the lack of understanding, the silence of things not talked about, allowed police to write off some of the women, and not look into their deaths and disappearances with the correct amount of urgency.

Like Eva's, other cases also seem to have had bafflingly little attention. As I have mentioned, many of the disappearances and deaths cluster around Christmas, a quiet time in Ireland, when people hole up at home. When someone with a job, say, might be more free to roam the country. Hunting. There's a plaque in Waterford city centre bearing the name of a twenty-two-year-old woman who went out one day around Christmas and never came home. Her family visit it, because they have no grave to go to. Imelda Keenan hasn't been seen in twenty-six years. She told her boyfriend Mark, whom she lived with, that she needed to buy cat litter and collect her dole cheque. It was 1.30 p.m. on 3 January 1994, just a few days into the new year, and she never came back. There were tip-offs, of course: someone said they'd seen a girl like Imelda getting on a train that day, from the station where her brother Ned in fact worked, but it could never be proved it was her. As in so many of these triangle cases, a suffocating silence has covered her disappearance. Someone must know how a young woman could vanish off the streets of a city in the middle of the day. But no one is talking. In 2019 her family, led by another of her brothers, Gerard, spoke out, making an appeal for more information. Nothing. There's always nothing.

Imelda was wearing leopard-print leggings that day, a denim jacket, white jumper. She had left her glasses at home, although she normally wore them – is that significant? Or just one of those tiny actions that mean nothing, except for the fact you did them on the last day you were ever seen? It was a bank holiday, so she couldn't have got her dole cheque in any case – did she just make a mistake with the dates, or does it mean something more? She had washed her hair that morning. Would she have done that anyway? She went out in the pouring rain. She was last seen near the Tower Hotel in Waterford, which was three minutes from her home, spotted by the receptionist from her local doctor's surgery. To get there from her flat she would have crossed the river, which at that time was very full, after days of heavy rain. Did she slip and fall in, unnoticed by anyone in the busy city centre? For some reason, like Eva Brennan's, Imelda's case was not included in the six that Operation Trace took on. So there's even less information about her than the others. She was walking by the river into town, and that was it. Nothing more.

I've struggled to find information about Imelda. She was strikingly pretty, with a wide smile, dark hair with a fringe. Blue eyes.

She had just finished a computer course, had her whole life ahead of her. She liked reading, embroidery. Like several of the other missing women, she had lost a parent young – her father had died when she was ten, and she was the youngest of nine children. Her brother Ned recalls that the last time he saw her, just before Christmas that year, she seemed quiet, like something was up. It's easy maybe in hindsight to think of these things. Imelda didn't go home for Christmas that year – she told her mother she'd come to visit after, when it was quieter. In her flat she had a Christmas tree, with presents under it for her family, including the nieces and nephews she loved. Her mother Elizabeth treasured that last Christmas card she received from Imelda, because she never saw her again after that. Elizabeth has passed away now, as has one of Imelda's brothers, without knowing her fate.

One interesting point I found was that Imelda had an interest in CB radios. She used to call herself 'Moonlight Girl' when she used them. In the days before the internet, this was one way to meet people. A way strangers could come into your life, perhaps. She'd met her boyfriend Mark that way, and they were engaged, planning a wedding in a leisurely way. When I try to work out what happened to the missing women, my mind starts wandering to ideas like making contact with strangers over the radio. Taking lifts late at night. Staying in relationships with abusive men, sneaking out to meet them. Walking home alone through a deserted park. Keeping secrets from family and friends. I don't like this way of thinking, which seems to imply that there are actions you can take that make your murder, your disappearance, more likely. The same is often true when a child is hurt or goes missing – people ask, what were the parents doing? Did they bring this on themselves, somehow? Does that mean the rest of us will be safe, if only we follow the rules? Again think of the backlash in the Madeleine McCann case. We want to imagine people are in some way deserving of their fate, not that they were just unlucky; not that some predators will strike anywhere, at any time. The middle of the day. Your own home. Outside your front door, in broad daylight. Why shouldn't women be allowed to walk anywhere, talk to anyone? Why should this mean they get murdered? In Imelda's case, all she did was walk through a busy city, in the middle of the day. Yet still she was gone. That's all I can say about this disappearance, which seems to have slipped from people's memories even more thoroughly than those of the other women.

I don't know why Imelda Keenan wasn't included in Operation Trace, the task force later set up to look at these disappearances – the Trace detectives didn't know either, and had simply been told to look at six cases and no others. Perhaps because Imelda lived slightly further away, not around Dublin, although it wasn't that far, only a two-hour drive. Certainly the police were aware of her disappearance, coming just a few days into January, after a year in which two women were already missing and a third murdered, all within an hour's distance of each other. It's hard not to conclude that indifference meant some of these disappearances weren't given enough attention. Either because the wrong assumption was made, or because the case simply slipped between the cracks. Perhaps there was even a general apathy among police to the fact that the cases were mounting up.

I had the benefit of hindsight, of course, but when I realised there had been so many just in the first year of the disappearances, I did feel shocked. And yet there was no enquiry, and no one officially linked the cases until much later. Eva's sister said she was dismissed by Gardaí when she suggested there might be a connection with another missing woman from just four months before, so close geographically. In the case of Marie Kilmartin, the existence of a suspect, and the circumstances of the disappearance, indicate that it's perhaps not linked to the triangle cases after all, but given how and where her body was buried, so similar to other women found dead in the years before, it's astonishing that links were not drawn sooner. Based on everything I've seen, I do think Eva and Imelda might have been abducted by a stranger, pulled into a car maybe as they walked along. There is a silence in the media about it too: although there are dozens of articles about Annie McCarrick, there are far fewer about Eva or Imelda or even Marie, murdered so brutally. Indifference can be fatal. Until we treat every case, every unsolved murder and every suspicious disappearance as equally important, we can't hope to build up a true picture of what killers are doing. That's how they get away with it.

Chapter Five

SEX AND SHAME

As I dug deeper into the social history of this time, the mid-nineties, it struck me just how much change took place in this five- or six-year period. Contraception legalised, divorce permitted, state-shaking debates over abortion. Paedophile priests arrested, homosexuality and suicide decriminalised, marital rape criminalised. Also, in 1993, the full horror of the Magdalene Laundries had begun to emerge, when mass graves were exhumed on the site of a former institution, which in true 1990s Dublin style was being sold for luxury flats. There were 155 women found buried there, but only death certificates for half of them, and many could not be named or traced. The Gardaí thought some of the women had died as recently as the late eighties. Thanks to several films and TV shows, such as *Philomena* and *The Magdalene Laundries*, the practice of sending pregnant girls to mother and baby homes is fairly well known outside Ireland. What's less well known is that these establishments didn't close down until quite recently – several were still open during the nineties, and the last one in Ireland shut in 1996. I think this says something about attitudes to unmarried mothers in Ireland at the time of these disappearances.

Also during this time, in 1996, it emerged that more than 2,000 Irish babies had been forcibly adopted over the years and given to American couples, often those barred from adopting in their own country, and often for sizeable donations to the Church (the same happened in other Catholic countries, such as Spain). Sometimes, the women would live with their babies in the homes for up to two years, only to find out that they were being taken away in a matter of hours. Often paperwork was forged, or the births mis-registered, the mother's name left off the certificate. The 2017 discovery of children's bodies at one mother and baby home in Tuam shows that the nuns were not above failing to register births at all, and that standards of care were often shocking.

The children torn from their mothers were the lucky ones – in some homes, the mortality rate was as high as 60 per cent. Hundreds of babies died, most without official records. Legal cases are currently making their way through the system to try to address this gross injustice, and in 2019 a UN special rapporteur commented that a full investigation was needed. Yet another tribunal, perhaps, to dissect Ireland's murky past. Interestingly, the special rapporteur specifically mentioned the 'culture of silence' that pervades Ireland. Both about the atrocities of the past, and the ongoing sexual abuse and violence against women. By not talking about these events, and in some cases by making sure there was no paper trail, terrible damage was done, and covered up for decades.

So sex, and shame about sex, was a big issue in Ireland in the nineties. As we've seen, the Child X case reminded us that the government felt it owned women's bodies, even those of children who had been raped. Parents would send you out of the room if something racy came on TV, periods had to be scrupulously hidden even in my all-girls school, and the nuns reminded us daily that sex was something for marriage. Priests thundered from the pulpits about the relaxing of sexual morals. At the same time, the hypocrisy was stunning. The Bishop of Galway was exposed in 1992 as having a secret son – this scandal added yet more cracks to the image of the Church in Ireland, already damaged by the child abuse revelations. I remember being sent out of the room yet again when it was discussed, seeing the book about the affair, written by the child's mother, on sale in Eason's in Newry and sneaking a peek inside. Just months before, this same bishop, Eamonn Casey, had publicly condemned the loosening of sexual morality in Ireland. The woman he had the affair with, Annie Murphy, was sent to a mother and baby home, and pressured to give up her son for adoption, but she refused. Incidentally, I was checking the facts of this on the final round of edits on the book, when I learned that Eamonn Casey was also accused of abusing several young girls over several decades from the seventies, including his niece, who was five at the time. He admitted abusing one of them, and two women were paid compensation by the Church. I think the fact I didn't even know this shows how entirely widespread the culture of abuse, and silence about abuse, was at the time. Casey died in 2017 without ever facing criminal charges, although the police were apparently aware of it from 2001 onwards.

Also in the nineties, another well-known priest, who'd also spoken out in the media about sexual morality, was found to have had two children with his housekeeper, one of whom had been put up for adoption. The other one was openly living with them. It says so much about how these men denounce others, while hiding away their own lovers and children, disposing of them like embarrassing secrets, and people did not take kindly to the revelations. It hardly seems a coincidence that the TV show *Father Ted*, which made fun of the clergy in a way that was affectionate but clear-eyed, began in 1995.

There was some progress in the nineties too – for example, being gay was finally legalised in Ireland. It's hard to believe this happened as late as 1993 but it did. But there was still a long way to go: a 2007 survey found that Ireland was the third most homophobic country in the western world. Northern Ireland was the second. In other social shifts, the magazine *Playboy* was finally allowed on sale in Ireland (progress!) and a referendum vote allowed divorce, finally, though it wouldn't become law until 1997. Non-Irish people never believe me when I say this, but it's true: you couldn't get divorced in Ireland until 1997. Ireland also had a female President, Mary Robinson, as of 1990. A human rights lawyer, she had fought for women's rights, for example legalising contraception in the Republic, which only became fully available in 1992. The role of President is largely ceremonial in Ireland, but there was no denying that this was progress, and I remember how inspiring it felt as a young girl to see a woman at the helm. Especially as the rest of Irish politics was a complete garbage-fire throughout the nineties: the government had collapsed in 1992 over a Watergate-style wire-tap scandal, leading to many years of unstable coalitions, surprise elections and endless tribunals over various scandals (BSE, contaminated blood, corruption, financial skulduggery and tax evasion, to name but a few). Not to mention referendums – Ireland had nine in the nineties alone. The country began to feel like a semi-failed state, the image of a warm, welcoming, wholesome place gone for ever, in its place a land ruled by corruption, cruelty and deep hypocrisy. Even though I vaguely remember a lot of this happening at the time – being sent out of the room notwithstanding – it was still surprising to group it together and realise how turbulent these years must have been, centuries of religious dogma swept away in less than a decade. I wondered what, if any, impact the prevailing attitudes, and this general air of chaos, had on the cases of the missing women.

As we've already seen, in late 1995 Jo Jo Dullard was most likely abducted while hitch-hiking home after missing her bus. This was partly caused by her lack of safe transport options. But there's more to the story than that. The family weren't happy with the initial police response, and this only got worse when someone from the local Gardaí leaked the fact that Jo Jo had a few weeks before travelled to England to have an abortion. They took it on themselves to speculate that she might have been suicidal as a result, although nothing in her behaviour suggested that was the case. Did the Gardaí make a massive assumption – that ending an unwanted pregnancy would make a woman want to die, or run away from her life? In a country like Ireland, where abortion only became legal in 2020, more than twenty years on, there's no way this could not have coloured people's views of Jo Jo. Maybe the police thought it more likely she went off with a man, if she was the kind of girl who'd get pregnant out of marriage. Maybe they didn't look as hard as they could have. Her family were furious, pointing out that she had plans for the future, she was going to learn to drive, she'd just taken up aerobics and was moving home to be near her sisters, her nieces and nephews. She wasn't depressed. What's more likely, that a young woman in fine spirits disappeared while hitch-hiking at night, in the same area where at least three women had already gone missing, or that she killed herself in some way such that her body has never been found? The fact that a police officer would even think such a thing speaks volumes about the attitude taken in many of these cases.

2018, as we've seen, was a year of two brutal murders in Ireland, of a young woman and a teenage girl. It was also the year the abortion referendum passed. I think it's worth pointing out that the 'eighth' – the amendment to the constitution that banned abortion in all cases, and which the repeal campaign successfully fought to overturn – was only introduced in 1983. This led to the country having some of the most restrictive abortion laws in the world; even though there was some leeway for doctors to perform one if a woman's life was in danger, they often would not do so, afraid of prosecution. This was shown with the death of Savita Halappanavar in Ireland in 2012. It was an agonising case: she knew that she was having an unavoidable miscarriage and that she was dying too, and still nothing was done for her. She asked repeatedly for doctors to help hasten the miscarriage before she developed sepsis, but they refused, and so she died. Her terrible death in large part led to the overturning of the eighth and the legalising of abortion.

At school, efforts to educate us against abortion were very muddled. I remember our religion teacher – because yes, we learned about sex in religion class – saying that the rhythm method was a very effective choice if you had to do something about 'all that'. This kind of wilful blindness had terrible consequences. In the late seventies, almost two-thirds of the population of Ireland were against the sale of contraceptives, and we had the highest birth rate in Europe. Contraceptives were banned, though wealthier people were often able to get them from friends overseas or lenient doctors. Visitors to the country were also not allowed to bring them in. It wasn't until 1992 – well into the AIDS crisis – that condoms became freely available. When I was a teenager, we knew sex was something to be afraid of. We knew we'd be judged for it, and that it might even kill us in the end. And until very recently, it was a shock to many in the rest of the UK to learn that abortion was also still illegal in Northern Ireland (along with gay marriage), and seemed likely to stay that way as long as there was no functioning government. This situation dragged on for some three years until a new government was formed in January 2020. Since March 2020 abortion is now officially legal in the North, although a woman went on trial as recently as July 2019 for buying pills online for her fifteen-year-old daughter. This is the context in which these disappearances and murders took place – a country where shame lingers even more than twenty years later, where women still do not have equal rights, where homophobia and intolerance remain rife.

A renewed appeal to find Jo Jo was launched as I was writing this book. A plaque was placed by the phone box where she made her last call. It reads: *Jo Jo Dullard, missing since 9 November 1995.*

What happened to her? Jo Jo's sister Mary, who fought tirelessly to find her, died in 2018. One of her brothers has also passed on. Her sister Kathleen keeps fighting as hard as she can. She says, 'We would be lucky to find her.' Meaning to find her body. That's all they hope for now, like so many of the families of the long-term missing – a body to bury. How sad that is. As well as Jo Jo's, there were other cases where judgement and shame surely played a factor in how thoroughly the women were looked for, how they were treated after their deaths. Marie Kilmartin, who'd had a child when she wasn't married. Layla Brennan, who was murdered in the triangle in 1999, and was painted in the press as a prostitute, a drug addict. I was shocked to find a newspaper headline from the time of her killer's trial, which read 'Life for Hooker Layla's Killer'. Why call her that? Why even mention that she did sex work – does it make any difference to the fact she was killed? Why do we judge the women who end up dead as if it's their own fault?

When I met Alan Bailey, one of the detectives in Operation Trace, he explicitly mentioned that when a woman went missing, judgements were often made about her past life and her sexual history. The focus of the investigation would often begin with the idea she'd gone off with a man, and not consider that perhaps she'd been taken against her will, as police might in America or England. You would think, 'Who's she gone away with?', is what Alan said. Judgement would start, and who knows what difference that makes to an investigation in those crucial early days? This attitude was confirmed by another retired Garda I spoke to, Pat Marry. Pat worked on many high-profile Irish murder cases, including that of Marilyn Rynn, and is now a private detective and author. He also worked on another of the triangle cases – the youngest missing woman, who was just seventeen when she disappeared, Ciara Breen.

I can't help drawing links between my life and Ciara Breen's. After all, I turned sixteen the year she was last seen, so we were almost the same age, and she lived in Dundalk, a town on the border, which is just twenty miles from where I grew up. We even used to go to some of the same discos – but do I need to say again that I have no memory from the time of hearing about her case? She went missing on 13 February 1997. At my convent school, girls would have been excited, getting ready for Valentine's Day flower deliveries. Many of the boyfriends sending the flowers would have been older, some a lot older. Grown men with cars and jobs. It was more accepted at the time, girls dating much older men. Ciara Breen was seventeen and lived alone with her mother, Bernadette, in a place called Bachelor's Walk in Dundalk, a block of terraced houses in the middle of town and just off a main road, surrounded by narrow lanes. Not a quiet spot by any means. If nobody saw anything that night, it would be surprising. Her grandparents lived just around the corner, in fact, and were well known in town – Ciara's great-grandfather and great-uncle had been TDs for the area, the equivalent of an MP. When I was a teenager, we didn't go to Dundalk very often. My parents considered it dangerous, which is ironic given we lived in Northern Ireland, and it was in the supposedly safer South. Situated as it was right on the border, a certain lawlessness had crept into the town, an overspill of violence, the smuggling of drugs and arms, the effect of the Troubles seeping down. Many border towns feel like this, and in Ireland it was even more evident. It's possible that Ciara was swept up in it.

Ciara was Bernadette Breen's only child, after her short-lived marriage had broken down. Her father lived in America, where he'd moved before Ciara was born. She had never met him, but over the previous year there had been discussion about making contact. He was due to come back to Ireland for a wedding, and there had been talk of Ciara meeting him then. That may have been on Ciara's mind at the time, causing worry and stress. She was also concerned about some dental work she had to have done – she'd always been self-conscious about her teeth, and would sometimes cover her mouth with her hand when speaking. In fact her front teeth had been extracted and not yet replaced when she went missing – an odd time for someone to run away. She had plans, a life to live. She was studying, she was going to go on holiday, she was maybe about to meet her father for the first time. Someone took all that away from her, and deprived her mother of her only child, left her to wonder, tormented, for the next twenty years. In 2004 Ciara, since she was under eighteen at the time she went missing, was included in a website of missing children launched in Ireland. That year, aged-up pictures of her were released by police and a large reward of 100,000 euros offered by Crimestoppers. Nothing changed.

At the time Ciara would also have been worried about her mother Bernadette, who was due to go to Dublin the next morning for the results of some cancer tests. Ciara and her mum had discussed the results, each trying to stay positive. That night, the two ate out at an Italian restaurant in town, then watched a film together – *Bad Boys* – and after that they chatted, and went off to bed around midnight. Ciara recorded *Circle of Friends* on video off the TV, as I probably would have done myself – the book was one of my favourites. I can picture her doing what I would have done, writing the title carefully on to a strip of masking tape, sticking it on to the video's spine in case someone would record over it. Practices that are dead and gone now, twenty years later. Two hours after they went to bed, Bernadette got up to use the bathroom, and noticed that Ciara was not in her bedroom. The window to her ground-floor room was on the latch, as if waiting for her to climb back in.

Bernadette stayed up all night, ready to scold her daughter, but Ciara never returned. The next day Bernadette's father drove her to Dublin for her appointment, where she was told that she did, as feared, have cancer. This news was overshadowed by her growing worry for her daughter, and on the way home she first voiced her fear to her father – Ciara had not come home that night. Quickly, it became clear that Ciara must have slipped out of her bed, into the dark and cold of a February night, to meet someone. Perhaps that person killed her. Perhaps someone else intercepted her on the way. I wondered if the fact that Ciara probably went out to meet someone clouded her case, as Jo Jo Dullard's abortion may have done for hers, and Eva Brennan's depression for hers. If people thought that she'd put herself in harm's way by sneaking out, maybe it changed the way they looked for her, the way they saw her. Ciara had run away before, after all, during a time when she'd fallen in with some wilder girls and begun to fight with her mother, as most teenage girls do. At first, Gardaí might have thought she'd done this again. Except – she hadn't taken anything with her this time. No money, no clothes, and no note left for her mother, despite the doctor's appointment in the morning.

When Ciara went missing she was wearing the typical clothes of a teenage girl in nineties Ireland. Childlike almost, not what would be considered sexy. We all wore sportswear, regardless of whether we did any sports (I certainly didn't), and jeans, baggy T-shirts and jumpers. What would be called normcore nowadays, now it's back in fashion. Ciara, who'd been to Florida a few months before and loved it, wore a leather jacket that night, with jeans and a T-shirt from Seaworld (I had one of these myself from when I'd gone with my parents in 1993 and again in 1995; this was before we realised it was cruel). She also wore a Mickey Mouse watch commemorating the 1994 World Cup in Florida, which many Irish people, including my uncle, had travelled over to, delighted that such a small country had managed to qualify again, after reaching the quarter-finals in 1990. What Ciara didn't know was that her mother was taking her to Florida once more for her eighteenth birthday in six weeks' time, as a surprise. She would never know what had been planned, because she was never seen again. In the main picture released to the press of her (unsmiling, maybe because of her teeth), she looks to be at Disneyland, perhaps in front of the 20,000 Leagues ride.

At first, there was a widespread search for Ciara, stretching as far as Warrenpoint in Northern Ireland, just north of the border. I was surprised to see this place mentioned in the reports, because it's two miles from where I grew up, a place I hung out a lot at this age, and yet I don't remember hearing anything about the search, or that a girl was even missing. Again, the border might have played a role in this. Gardaí then found out she'd met a boy from Kilkeel, which is also near where I grew up. This boy was traced, but had not seen Ciara since their encounter at a disco. A week after the disappearance, a man rang the house looking for Ciara. He told her mother he'd seen her at the same disco on Valentine's night – the day after she went missing – and that she'd got a lift home with another girl. Nothing came of this and it's likely he got the dates wrong, as happened in many of these other cases, well-meaning people trying to help but unwittingly sending the investigation in the wrong direction. By the way, I think this was the same disco I used to go to myself. It's possible I even walked past Ciara without knowing it, waited beside her for a lift home, shivering in the cold, because we never wore coats.

Ciara was known to be friendly with a group of wilder girls, and it was with one of them that she'd tried to run away the previous year. She'd hidden in a house in Armagh, in Northern Ireland, but had been found after a week – it seemed she hadn't enjoyed the experience much. These girls helped the police as much as they could, pointing towards an older man who'd shown an interest in Ciara. Bernadette recalled seeing this same man chatting up Ciara – then only sixteen – on their doorstep the year before. Bernadette, who was at the time thirty-eight, described the man as being closer to her own age than her daughter's. Gardaí later found out that he'd perhaps been seeing Ciara for some time, maybe a year. He'd also had relationships with other young girls, and had been possessive and sometimes violent, even stalking them. Rumours abounded about this man. That he'd told other girls he would put them in the bog, like he had with Ciara. But when Gardaí tried to search the wet, marshy bog land around Dundalk, they found tons of illegally dumped building waste, which meant they couldn't carry on with the operation as the ground was too contaminated. The suspect was seen loitering nearby a few times, watching their progress. I've seen pictures of the investigations and the land is completely overgrown, waterlogged – it would be very easy to hide a body there and never have it surface.

When I spoke to Pat Marry, the retired Garda who worked on Ciara's case, he told me that yes, Ciara had been seen as 'wayward'. The police knew she'd been in a relationship with this older man, and likely been sleeping with him for some time. Nowadays we'd say he was grooming her, but such things weren't well understood in the nineties. Pat was also sure he knew who Ciara's killer was. In 1999, the man she was seeing was arrested and questioned about the case but released without charge after several days. In 2014 police in Dundalk received an anonymous tip off, via a series of letters, that this same man had definitely been involved in Ciara's death and had even boasted about it. That man, who was thirty-four when Ciara went missing, twice her age, can be named, because he's dead. Liam Mullen killed himself in police custody in 2017, by taking an overdose just after he was arrested for drink-driving. He died still denying he'd done anything to Ciara.

Ciara's mother, Bernadette, died in 2018. In her final years, she had the repeated pain of believing her daughter might be found. Not alive; she had accepted that Ciara was dead. All she wanted was a body to bury, something that for Irish Catholic people is a deep and spiritual need. Several more searches of the bogs around the border area yielded nothing definite, although Pat says they found some clothing that may well have belonged to Ciara. He was convinced that it did, but her mother was too overwhelmed to make a positive ID. Who can blame her, when admitting that these were her daughter's clothes in the bog would mean Ciara was probably dead? There was a brief moment of hope when bones were found years later at a house just metres from where Ciara lived – but these proved to be historical remains. It's hard to imagine how this felt for Bernadette Breen, after twenty years of searching, to have her hopes dashed like that. Or that her hopes even centred around finding her beloved daughter's bones. When she died, she was not even seventy. She spoke of her frustration when the suspect died without ever saying where Ciara was, but said she had also prayed for him, leaning hard into her faith.

I find it striking that Ciara, as close as she was to her mother, was keeping secrets from her, perhaps for as long as a year. Secrets pervade Irish culture as we've seen, and I can't help linking this damaging silence to the shame and guilt of the Catholic Church, the treatment of sexuality. If you knew you would be pilloried for having a relationship, perhaps you would keep it a secret. In the nineties, most people would have known a woman who'd been punished for slipping up sexually, who'd had her child taken away and adopted perhaps, maybe even been sent to a Magdalene Laundry, or a family where the youngest child was in fact a grandchild. Secrets. Silence. They were everywhere.

Jo Jo and Ciara's cases made me think of another one, from the same year Jo Jo went missing but which, unlike hers, dominated the news worldwide. The links between Ireland and America are strong and well documented. For example, until 9/11, when the true impact of terrorism was felt on American soil, the IRA was being extensively funded by American Irish Republicans who had often never set foot in the country. When Bill Clinton came to visit Belfast in 1995, it was a big deal – he was loved almost as much as that revered Irish American President, JFK. But also in 1995, Bill Clinton was complicit in the silencing and shaming of Monica Lewinsky. We knew all about this, giggling at it in school without totally understanding the details. She was a joke, a slapper, a silly girl. I was thirteen at the time, and I didn't entirely get what it was he'd done to her, but knew she had been degraded in some way, had let him ruin her and it was her fault. It's only as an adult that I see it for what it was – a terrible abuse of power from a much older man, the most powerful man in the world, to a young subordinate woman – she was only twenty-two years old at the time. She has said since that their relationship was consensual, but she has been paying for it ever since. So maybe this story wasn't what we thought – a jokey, sleazy tale, a convenient excuse to rock a presidency, but a young woman put in an impossible position by a man who let her life be ruined, her reputation savaged, while his was largely unscathed. Monica Lewinsky's story echoes what was happening in Ireland at the same time – so many children and women silenced, their abuse ignored in favour of protecting the men who run everything. Priests, politicians, IRA commanders, all the same.

It was clear from my research, and talking to Pat Marry, that Ciara Breen's disappearance was actually not a mystery, it had just never been officially solved. I asked Pat then – since it was fairly obvious who'd killed Ciara, and he wasn't in the frame for any of the other cases – if it was a mistake to include her in Operation Trace, the cold-case review. Of course it was, said Pat. It clouded the waters, and wasted time, took the focus from the real killer, who-ever that was. For me this was a new way of looking at the triangle cases. I'd been building up the impression that the Gardaí had been negligent in not linking the cases sooner, but maybe they weren't all linked after all. Here was one where there was a clear suspect, and yet he had never been charged with the crime and now it was too late. I started to wonder how that could happen – and had it happened in any of the other cases?

Chapter Six

OTHER FACTORS

The more I learned about just how many cases there were in the nineties, the more I wondered. How could so many women go missing from the same area – Annie, Eva, Imelda, Jo Jo, making four by the end of 1995, along with the unsolved murder of Marie Kilmartin – and there be no national outcry, no task force or even a suggested link between them? Maybe I was being too harsh on the police – maybe there were reasons not to link the cases. For a start, people disappear a lot more often than we realise. In the UK, something like 1,000 people are reported missing every day. Most of them will quickly be found – around 99 per cent within a year – but that still leaves a significant number who can't be located.

Then there's the sheer lack of evidence. No crime scenes, no forensics and of course no body to even prove a woman was dead. It's very hard to convict someone of murder with no body; one of the first times this happened in the UK was an IRA victim, an undercover soldier considered one of the 'Disappeared'; that is, people who were murdered by terrorists, mostly in the seventies, and their bodies hidden. There were originally sixteen names on the list, but two more were added in the 2000s. Although Captain Robert

Nairac's body has still not been found, along with two others of the original sixteen, several people were convicted of his murder in the seventies. As part of my research, I spoke to Darren Boyle, who's spent many years working in crime journalism in both Ireland and England, and is very well acquainted with the triangle cases. He pointed out that most murderers have no idea they're going to kill, and no plan for what to do afterwards when they suddenly have a body on their hands. They are impulse crimes, and therefore hard to cover up. Usually, in an unplanned crime, there's blood, fingerprints, fibre evidence and, nowadays, phone records and a digital trail as well. In these triangle cases, the fact that no bodies have ever been found suggests someone organised, someone who went out ready to kill that day, or perhaps even two people working together. Of the women who were murdered in the same area, whose cases are possibly linked, many were found buried deep in the bog, far from the road, which suggests you might need more than one person to carry them there. Darren is not the first to mention this theory, of joint murderers. I wondered what kind of person would know how to hide a body so well, and to avoid leaving any other evidence. Would be able to take a woman off the street, sometimes in the middle of the day, without even being seen. Someone who'd done it before?

Another important fact is that these disappearances took place just before the technological revolution that changed all our lives. Most people in Ireland did not have mobile phones until the very end of the decade, so if you saw something suspicious and wanted to ring the police you would have to find a payphone, not all that common in the countryside, and try to get change and hope the phone was working. I was shocked to learn recently that as many as 20 per cent of people in the UK never use the internet (according to a 2019 survey). Living in the city where food, Ubers and friends can be summoned with one click of your smartphone, it's easy to forget that. Darren also pointed out that not having mobile phones makes a huge difference to how easy it is to find people when they're lost – our every move is now tracked, as you learn when you get the surprise of looking up a place you know you once went to in the distant past, and Google tells you the exact date. In many of the triangle cases, without that technology, police were just guessing a woman's last movements, when or if events occurred, or relying on witnesses who, as we've seen, often mixed up key dates, or didn't come forward for months or even years. The search area was huge and confused. In the nineties, there was also a lack of CCTV. It was easy to vanish, or to make someone vanish.

As well as these factors, a key one is that DNA testing was not available until the mid-nineties, and even then Ireland lagged behind in the availability of testing facilities. One earlier case, the first featured in this book, illustrates perfectly the difference DNA makes. Phyllis Murphy was a young woman who went missing in 1979 while out Christmas shopping. Her body was later found dumped in the Wicklow Mountains, her gifts and possessions scattered around the countryside. When Phyllis was first found dead, one suspect was a local man named John Crerar, a father of five and a former soldier, with no previous convictions. Despite this, he was on the Gardaí's radar from the beginning, as he'd lied in an interview and said he didn't know Phyllis, when in fact his family had lived near hers when he was young – her sisters (she was one of ten children) had even babysat for him. Crerar voluntarily gave a blood sample to the Gardaí, as did dozens of other local men; of course this was of limited use back in 1979 but it could sometimes be used to match semen samples. No one could have known how DNA would soon transform investigations; at the time he must have thought there was little chance it could be used against him. Besides, he knew that Phyllis's body had been left out for a month before she was found, and perhaps he thought no trace of him would remain after that long. In fact, it was unusually cold that year, and the sample was quite well preserved.

Luckily, a tenacious officer kept the case in mind for twenty years, and when DNA testing became available, he sent the sample off to a lab in England for analysis. Ireland had no such facilities at the time, and even sending it to the UK caused issues with the budget. There was some debate over whether this set of samples would be tested at all. It took several months to get the results, but everything pointed straight to John Crerar, the man they'd discounted because he supposedly had an alibi. Luckily that one Garda – a man named Christy Sheridan – had had the foresight twenty years earlier to lock away the samples taken from local men and keep the key, as if anticipating that one day they would be needed again. The Gardaí went to John Crerar's door, this man who'd led an apparently blameless life, and arrested him for a murder committed twenty years before. This was in 1999, although it would be another three years before he was convicted at trial. What did he do during those intervening years, the eighties and nineties, when so many women went missing or were murdered? Phyllis's body was found only twenty miles from where Annie McCarrick was last seen, for example, and even closer to where Antoinette Smith and Patricia Doherty were buried. Could there really have been more than one man killing women and dumping them in this small patch of mountains during this time?

DNA testing didn't really come in until the early nineties, and has grown much more sophisticated since then. More than one cold case has been solved this way in recent years.

The first to be solved by DNA analysis in Ireland was, as we've seen, the murder of Marilyn Rynn, who was raped and strangled after taking a shortcut home after a night out, in fact on the same day as Phyllis Murphy but sixteen years later. It wasn't until August 1996, eight months later, that the man who attacked Marilyn – David Lawler – was arrested. He was found during house-to-house searches, when Pat Marry, the Garda who worked on the case, noticed that he told a small lie about where he was that night. Like John Crerar, he gave a blood sample voluntarily. It's hard to know why he would do this, when he didn't have to – maybe he thought, again like Crerar, that the DNA would not have survived that long outside (the Gardaí also found that he'd looked up the question online; as a telecoms engineer he was an early adopter of the internet). However, his luck was out: it was again very cold that winter, so the body was preserved where it lay in undergrowth, near the path Marilyn had taken, and the DNA with it. As it was, it took five months to have the samples analysed, since they didn't have the facilities in Dublin, and when the results came back he was charged then bailed. I find this extraordinary – it's very unusual to be let out on bail for a violent crime, let alone murder. Especially with such strong evidence. The case didn't come to trial for almost two years, during which he was free to live his life. By that time, his wife was pregnant with their second child. This is also hard to fathom – maybe she thought he was innocent, despite the DNA evidence. The fact remains that she conceived a child with him after he'd been charged with rape and murder.

Several more recent cases in Ireland have been solved either by DNA or technology or both. For example there's Elaine O'Hara, murdered in 2011: her killer would be captured when his phone SIM cards were found discarded, another sign of the role technology has to play in catching these predators. Elaine was thirty-six and worked in childcare. Again, she was assumed to have killed herself before her body was found, as she was known to have been unhappy, and had spent time in a psychiatric hospital. She had last been seen at her mother's grave, possibly crying. However, about a year after she went missing, her handbag was found in a reservoir in Wicklow, since the water had dried up after an unusually hot summer. Two mobile phones were also found, as well as a bondage mask, a rope and knife, and several sex toys. A few days later, a dog walker found Elaine's body about forty minutes away from the handbag's location – she had been stabbed. The phones showed that Elaine had been seeing a man called Graham Dwyer, who was into BDSM and had expressed a desire to stab a woman while having sex. He was unanimously convicted of killing Elaine, but as in recent cases where BDSM has been used as a defence, her family had to endure listening to talk about her sexual preferences and history, while she wasn't there to speak for herself. If not for mobile-phone evidence, Elaine's death might well have been labelled a suicide, and her killer gone free, perhaps to do it again.

The next year, in 2012, a woman named Aoife Phelan was killed, strangled by a man she was in a relationship with, Robert Corbet. He used a plastic bag secured with cable ties, like Larry Murphy had done back in 2000, then put her body in a barrel, getting some unsuspecting friends to help him bury it, saying it was full of oil. He might easily have got away with it, and Aoife joined the lists of missing persons, had CCTV not captured some of what he did. Both these murders took place in the triangle area, but Gardaí were not able to find any links to the earlier disappearances, and Corbet for one was too young to have been involved. However, both these murders show how the nineties cases might well have been solved if they'd happened a few years later. It's hard to imagine so many women going missing without a trace now, when our mobiles map out our every step, when most of the country is covered in CCTV, when everyone can call the police right away when they see something suspicious happen. For example, if Annie McCarrick had gone missing later on, it's likely there would have been CCTV on the bus she took. She probably would have texted to arrange her day out, leaving an electronic trail. There would have been CCTV in the pub, if that was her, and probably in the car park if she left with someone. Other drinkers that night might have taken pictures that captured her in the background (in fact there were a few pictures taken on cameras that night, although they didn't yield any useful clues). In some ways, the triangle women were unlucky to disappear just before the technological revolution, if we can say there are degrees of luck even among the murdered.

I've previously looked at the way indifference, or lack of interest, seemed to play a part in some of the disappearances not being solved. I think silence also has a role. The silence of judgement, of making assumptions about why a woman died or what happened to her. The silence of shame – women not telling those closest to them that they were involved with a man, as happened with Ciara Breen. The silence of fear – not speaking out because the suspect perhaps had dangerous connections, or because people in Ireland don't trust the police, maybe because of our political situation. Witnesses who didn't report what they'd seen for months, or reported the wrong thing through simple error. Sometimes, however, this goes even further, and people actually lie to the police. In some cases this has allowed brutal killers to go free.

The issue of false alibis comes up in a number of these cases. For example that of Patricia Furlong, who was strangled in a field in 1982. This was another case with an obvious suspect: a well-known DJ, Vincent Connell, was seen with her just before she died, but he managed to get his girlfriend at the time to give him a false alibi. She was too frightened to contradict him when he said, in front of police, that he'd been with her all night; he had a long history of hurting the women he dated, and after Patricia's death he moved to South Africa, where the abuse continued. He left one woman chained to a radiator while he went to work, and choked another till she passed out. If a girlfriend ever found the courage to leave, he said he'd kill her family, and indeed he did set fire to the house of one ex's parents, not once but twice. He'd even made plans to rape the same woman's mother with a curling iron, allegedly paying someone two grand to do it, a huge amount of money in those days, but the man he paid said he couldn't go through with it when he saw the lady at her door. Eventually, when Connell had returned to Ireland, his alibi fell apart after his former girlfriend told the truth, and he was convicted of killing Patricia. This was in 1991; however, he got out on appeal four years later. He died in 1998, meaning he would have been free for some of the triangle disappearances, though he always maintained he'd not harmed Patricia. At his appeal, the judge made a point of saying he was letting Vincent go in part because he spoke well and dressed nicely, he'd always worked hard and even raised money for charity, all of which seemed to count for more than the lives of the many women he'd terrorised, beaten and tortured. Perhaps he would have been convicted right away had his girlfriend not been so scared that she lied for him, or the police had better understood coercion and not interviewed them in the same room. If so, dozens of women would have been spared great pain.

In the case of John Crerar, who murdered Phyllis Murphy and got away with it for twenty years, an important factor in him not being caught sooner was that a colleague lied for him. This man said Crerar had been at work during the time Phyllis went missing, when in fact he'd been an hour late that day, and had then quickly left again and come back almost two hours after that. The man didn't want to get Crerar into trouble – there was some suggestion he thought he was helping his colleague hide an affair. He'd lied even when he saw Crerar scrubbing out his car with boiling water that day, acting suspiciously and carrying kettle after kettle over to do it. He'd spilled some milk in there, Crerar said. The man apparently believed him, lied to the police, and so Crerar remained free for twenty years. It later emerged that two young girls, one just ten at the time, had also accused Crerar of sexual assault years before, but nothing was ever done about it. So an apparently spotless record doesn't always mean that, when you look a little closer.

I want to say a few things here about what we can learn from these two cases, and why they weren't prosecuted sooner or more successfully. First, there is the factor of people lying, giving false alibis. In one case, a man was helping out a work friend, keeping him out of trouble with the bosses and his wife, thinking there was no harm in it. If it wasn't for the colleague retracting John Crerar's alibi, as well as DNA testing becoming available (and some good police work), it's easy to imagine Phyllis's murder remaining unsolved. Perhaps someone has been lying in the cases of the missing women, who might hold the key to what happened. In the other case, a woman was too afraid to speak out against her violent boyfriend. Alan Bailey told me that he believed a breakthrough in one or more of these cases might come if a woman found the courage to talk, if a man she had been afraid of was finally gone from her life. Another factor, which I've discussed before, is the need for earlier, more minor offences to be caught, reported and prosecuted sooner. Vincent Connell had attacked so many women by the time Patricia died that he must have thought he'd always get away with it, as indeed he did for the most part. Even if he didn't kill Patricia, his record is shocking. As we've seen, many men who kill women have convictions in their past for the sexual assault of women and girls, even for murder in some cases. They often got off on some technicality, or got the crime downgraded to a lesser charge and so served no time, or only a short sentence and were soon free to continue their violent behaviour.

Another factor in some of these disappearances is surely the political turmoil in Ireland at the time. The years of the disappearances – 1993 to 1998 – were some of the most turbulent of all the Troubles. In 1993 a chip shop was blown up by the IRA in Belfast, killing children in the street. A week later a Catholic pub was shot up by the UDA in retaliation, eight murdered, never mind that those people were innocent too. I remember seeing it on the news, broken glass and blood everywhere, knowing that being a child was no protection, and neither was staying out of politics. The peace process rumbled on, with progress towards all-party talks, to include paramilitaries for the first time. A soldier who'd shot and killed a teenage girl in 1990 was released from prison after just two years. Bill Clinton came to visit in 1995, and his Secret Service agents reportedly enjoyed the doughnut bakeries of Belfast. At the same time, Gerry Adams told a rally that the IRA 'hadn't gone away, you know'. This sinister remark was endlessly lampooned. Even as the Troubles inched to the end, the terrible violence went on. It would hardly be surprising if the news didn't have enough room for missing women, or that the police were distracted. Shootings and bombings continued on a near-daily basis – on just one day in January 1998, when the Troubles were supposedly almost over, three people were shot in separate incidents, this in an area with a population of just a million. This daily onslaught ended in August that year, when the sheer horror of the Omagh bomb led most of the remaining dissident groups to announce ceasefires. Had peace finally been won by a last, terrible sacrifice of blood? Yet even after Omagh, there were still several sectarian killings. Peace has always been extremely fragile, as everyone in Northern Ireland knows and no one outside it seems to get.

I grew up a few miles from the border. You could cross it with ease by the late eighties, as by this point there was no physical machinery there. Many people did and still do live on one side, work on the other, their lives a complicated work-around of which country they pay taxes in and where they register their cars. Northern Ireland has always been a surreal place, both one thing and another. You're on the island of Ireland, and if you grew up where I did, the South is spitting distance away. You could stand with your feet on either side of the supposed border. If you wanted to post a letter over it, however, to a town just miles away, you needed a European stamp that was twice the price. Most families kept 'punt purses', later euro purses, for those occasions when something, like petrol, was cheaper on the other side of the border. Your mobile phone still gets confused at your parents' house, thinking it's in Ireland, switching back and forward several times an hour. In a way that's what the people do too, switch back and forward.

When I started writing my series of crime novels, I imagined a cross-border unit dedicated to finding missing persons. I had always been fascinated by the phenomenon, the sheer unknowing, the endless spool of questions, the fact they might still be alive somewhere. However, no such unit exists in Ireland, and in the nineties it was not even possible to extradite someone over the border, which might have meant simply driving a few miles down a road. A missing person could simply step over that imaginary line, or be taken over it, and become someone else's problem. This doesn't entirely make sense to me, the way that despite the flimsiness of this so-called border, it's treated like the Berlin Wall, as if a killer could not easily cross it, as if violence does not spill over. IRA suspects and paedophile priests were able to slip across it and remain at liberty, as we've seen; and there was a scandal in 2014 about IRA 'on-the-runs', terrorists who'd been living across the border for decades after escaping from the North.

In 1994, Arlene Arkinson's disappearance was complicated because it wasn't clear *where* she had gone missing, on which side of the border, and also possibly by the political connections of the man, Robert Howard, who in all likelihood killed her. There is evidence that he used to travel back and forward from Ireland to England using the ferries – there is still usually no passport control on this method of travel, so it's an easy way to slip into the country unnoticed. He had a car, he was in Ireland at the time, roaming about the country from town to town, and young women went missing around him. Robert Howard is dead now, so we can speculate. If Howard had gone on trial in Southern Ireland, the jury would have been told that since Arlene's disappearance, he'd murdered another teenage girl, and it's likely he would have been convicted of killing Arlene. Perhaps then her family would have had some answers, and her body might have been located. But we'll never know the answer. It took twenty-four years to hold an inquest into Arlene's death. Her body remains unfound. Her family remains in limbo. They have repeatedly called for a public enquiry into how the RUC managed to mess up the case quite so spectacularly, but then again it's hardly the only thing it bungled over the years (collusion, informers, corruption, you name it). The RUC was actually disbanded as part of the Good Friday Agreement, so completely tainted was it. In an indirect way, Arlene is another victim of the Troubles, caught up in the blizzard of other deaths, the bizarre political situation at the time, and the sheer lack of interest in what happened to a vulnerable teenage girl.

It's easy to forget that the porous border between Ireland and the UK isn't just the one between Northern and Southern Ireland, but on all routes between the two countries, ferries and even planes in some cases. On a recent trip to Ireland, I made it from Wales to Dublin to where my parents live in the North, to Donegal and back through the North to Dublin and then to Wales again. I didn't show ID at any point; indeed, it was hard to tell I had crossed a border at all. Perhaps this ease of travel is also a factor in the disappearances – a killer could easily move back and forward between Ireland, Northern Ireland and Great Britain. For example, there was a woman named Ellen Cross, who left Manchester in 1999 to take the ferry from Holyhead to Dublin, and never arrived; her family believe she made it as far as Dublin and went missing there, which would put her within the scope of the vanishing triangle, and could possibly suggest the disappearances of women continued even longer than thought. It was a very long time before I came across Ellen's name, as her case has largely been forgotten. Ellen was fifty, so maybe she doesn't fit the demographic, but shouldn't she be included? We have no real idea what the killer's 'type' was, or even if there was a single killer at all.

There were other violent men on the Gardaí's radar, who were known to have killed women in the UK but were able to cross the border and travel freely to Ireland, or vice versa. Martin Stafford died in prison in 2015, like Robert Howard, after being convicted of murdering a woman in Birmingham in 2004; he had spent time in Dublin, too, and was in fact originally from there. In 1997 he'd also gone to prison for abducting a woman at knifepoint but only served a few years, in yet another depressing example of warnings not being heeded. The woman he killed in England has never been found – when someone is extradited from Ireland to the UK, this can only be for the purpose of facing charges, so the police could not formally question him about the location of the body. Another example of the law acting in favour of the perpetrators, but also of how murder convictions can be secured even when a body hasn't been found. It shows, too, how easily someone could cross back and forward, slipping in and out of different jurisdictions as easily as boarding a ferry or driving down a road. Perhaps we need to think not in terms of a triangle around Dublin, but of two countries, Ireland and the UK, which a killer could move between with great ease, targeting women wherever they went. And even if such men were not directly involved in terrorism, they lived in a society saturated with it, where many people had experience of violent death, both causing it and covering it up. Perhaps that played a role too.

I began to wonder if the border had been a factor in Ciara Breen's disappearance. After all, she lived in a town just over it, and like me travelled back and forward across it for nights out and to see friends. Ciara went missing in 1997. We were then a few months away from the Labour victory that would finally bring an end to the violence I'd grown up surrounded by, with the Good Friday Agreement that would be signed in April 1998. I had big plans – voting as soon as I could, going to university, leaving this country for somewhere more exciting and less dangerous. Ironically, Northern Ireland suddenly became hip not long after I'd left for university, in 2000, but in the nineties it still felt like the end of the known universe, especially the small village where I grew up. In 1997 everything was still uncertain. Bombs were thrown, mortars and even rockets fired. On 12 February, the day before Ciara's disappearance, the IRA killed a soldier, supposedly the last one to die in the Troubles. However, as we've seen, the past doesn't always stay past in Northern Ireland, and more soldiers and police officers would die in the future, twelve years and more after the Troubles were apparently over. Two weeks after Ciara's disappearance, another young woman, aged just sixteen, was given a punishment beating by the IRA, her head shaved and paint poured over her as she was tied to a lamppost. Strangely, I don't recall ever hearing about this, although I was almost the same age and lived not far away.

A look at the timeline for 1997 alone shows the sheer number of bombing and shooting incidents that took place that year, several a week sometimes. Twenty people died in this, the last full year of the Troubles. The Grand National was even cancelled because of an IRA bomb threat. Billy Wright, leader of Loyalist terror group the LVF, was somehow shot dead by Republican paramilitaries while inside the Maze prison. A Catholic man was beaten to death by a Loyalist mob, while RUC officers reportedly sat in a car nearby and watched. Another young Catholic woman, just eighteen, was shot in the head as she slept, probably by Loyalist terrorists. A week later, a sixteen-year-old Catholic boy was abducted, tortured and murdered, his body dumped in a pit of animal remains, again it was thought by the same Loyalist group.

Reading over this list of events, on the CAIN website, which catalogues every single incident of the Troubles, I realise that I have forgotten some part of being young in Northern Ireland, the non-stop nature of the violence, turning on the news every night waiting to see if someone else had been shot, if there'd been another bomb or abduction. It's overwhelming to see it written down, remember how many shootings and bombings took place every week. In among all this news, maybe the missing women just got forgotten. It's also notable that teenagers were not exempt from being drawn into the Troubles, and murdered. In Ciara's case, there was also the complication of two police forces having to work together, as she might have been on either side of the border. With all this going on, no wonder if her case didn't get the attention it deserved, or if mistakes were made, as Pat Marry, the retired Garda, feels.

I realised that not just the political ramifications of the border, but also its geography, maybe played a role in the disappearances. We know that several women were murdered in the mountains around Dublin, perfect for hiding bodies, remote and boggy. There are also large swathes of bog land around the border, where searchers for Ciara Breen's body were frustrated by the terrain, all rubbish and undergrowth and marsh. This area was also well known as a place where the IRA hid bodies. Some of the Disappeared, who were murdered in the seventies and eighties, were hidden in this borderland. In some cases, elaborate subterfuge, such as letters sent from England, made their families think they were still alive. The motive for this is unclear except for cruelty, sadism. As part of the peace process, an organisation was set up to try to find these bodies. The ICLVR, the Independent Commission for the Location of Victims' Remains, has a unique remit in that it collects information from former terrorists and uses it to find people. By law, it can't prosecute anyone as a result of information received – the idea is simply to retrieve the bodies for the families, and it has had great success. In 2003 the long-missing body of one of the Disappeared, Jean McConville, was found just half an hour's drive from where Ciara went missing. Jean was the only woman disappeared by the

IRA, back in 1972, and a major effort to find her had yielded nothing after several lengthy searches, only for her body to be uncovered accidentally by coastal erosion, spotted by walkers on a beach. She had been missing at this point for over thirty years, since she was taken by the IRA from her flat in Divis Towers, Belfast, in front of her children. Jean had ten children and the eldest was not even sixteen – she had been sent out to buy chips and when she came back her mother was gone, her siblings hysterical. Saying Jean was taken by the IRA seems to cover up a truth of the case: some of those who took her were her own neighbours in the flats, men and women known to the family. Indeed, her orphaned children still see these people around Belfast from time to time, something that many victims of the Troubles and their families just have to live with. Jean was a Protestant, who'd married a Catholic man. Her husband was dead, so she was living in poverty, coping with grief and what sounds like severe depression, with ten children, surrounded by people who were willing to kill her.

I had known Jean's story, of course – everyone did in Northern Ireland, an example of the IRA's callousness in taking away a widow with ten children, sometimes given by Catholics as a reason for not supporting them. It's a peculiarly Irish story, touching on so many of the country's past shames. The cruelty and evasions of the IRA, who had known for years what happened to her but wouldn't say. The accusations that Jean was a spy for MI5, which her children said were ludicrous. The fact she was 'disappeared' instead of simply being murdered, so the family had thirty years of not knowing what became of her. The abuse her orphaned children suffered, both physical and sexual, in the so-called religious homes they were sent to after they lost her. That they were split up and didn't see each other for years. The fact that Jean, who'd had fourteen births and ten surviving children, was only thirty-eight when she died. This particular aspect had eluded me somehow until quite recently. She married at nineteen and there was a set of twins in the family, but all the same she must have been near-constantly pregnant to have had fourteen children in eighteen years. It says so much to me about how women were treated in Catholicism, like cows to give birth over and over, in a country with no abortion. Contraception was at least available in Northern Ireland – it wouldn't be fully legal in the South until the nineties – but was frowned upon for Catholic families, spoken of as a sin.

Since 1999, when the commission was set up, thirteen of the original 'Disappeared' have been located, and three are still missing. However, if Ciara Breen is also buried in this troubled border area, this no man's land, as former Garda Pat Marry is convinced, she has yet to be found. Her case is still not solved, and now that her mother has gone, along with the chief suspect in her disappearance, it's likely that we'll never know what happened to the young girl who slipped out of her window on a February night more than twenty years ago. She would be thirty-nine now, had she not climbed out of that window on that particular night. Just a year older than me.

The success of the ICLVR shows that there is an approach that can work to find missing people – intensive searching of large areas, coupled with anonymous intelligence. The commission has resources, diggers, experienced searchers and scientists. Crucially, they can offer immunity to witnesses. And they find people. Might that be an idea for the triangle cases? To set up an anonymous tip-line and dig in the areas suggested? Of course, it means sacrificing so much. By law, no one can be prosecuted because of finds made by the ICLVR. It means giving up any thought of justice, trading that for the cold comfort of a body to bury. Many of the families, I think, would take the compromise if they could. In future, it's essential the police in Ireland find a way to work together, especially in cases where it's not clear on which side of the border a murder was committed. For years the border, and the political situation, have allowed people to escape from the terrible crimes they carried out either side of it, from the 'on-the-runs' of the IRA to the man who may have given a lift to Annie McCarrick that night. Too often we've behaved as if the border were a portal of some kind, expunging sins, allowing immunity from crimes. As if politics matters more than human lives, especially those of women and children. But Ireland is small, and the border is just a line. These men always resurface, and the lives of many women and children have been ruined because of such thinking, in some cases lost altogether.

So there's a host of other factors that may have played a role in the triangle disappearances. The lack of physical evidence, DNA testing, or technology. The fact that it's easy to hide bodies in boggy, remote areas of the country. The number of people willing to keep silent, or even lie – former Garda Alan Bailey is convinced that someone out there knows more about the disappearances than they've ever said. The sheer chaos of those years politically, with sectarian deaths every few days, a strained police force and the fact that the police in Northern Ireland, Southern Ireland and Great Britain often didn't share notes or acknowledge that essentially the borders were open during these years, and still are. All these issues may have meant the cases went unsolved. However, they didn't cause the disappearances – or murders, as they most likely are – in the first place. Only one thing caused that and it was this: a man, or more than one man, who was willing to kill women. As my research continued, I was having to face the extent of this in Ireland.

Chapter Seven

VIOLENCE AGAINST WOMEN

In 1996 I was fourteen, going to school every day in my bottle-green uniform, doing my homework, crushing long-distance over the boys who shared our school bus, a noxious cloud of Lynx Africa left in their wake. Every night we watched the news over dinner, and before I went to sleep I would say my prayers, as I'd been taught. Please let there be peace. Please let it end. It was also the year of the Drumcree stand-off, a faintly ridiculous protest involving Orangemen camping out in a field, that nonetheless showed how far we still had to go towards peace. A Guard was murdered by the IRA as far south of the border as Limerick, which again shows that violence is no respecter of borders. I spent the summer in the Gaeltacht in Donegal again, not far from where Arlene Arkinson had gone out on the night she went missing, and the weather was so bad we barely saw the huge mountain behind us for weeks. We joked that the Orangemen were holding it hostage.

Also in 1996, another woman would vanish in the triangle. Fiona Pender was twenty-five and seven months pregnant. Her family had been hit by tragedy already when her brother Mark was killed in a motorbike crash the year before, leaving behind a young son. Fiona, who also loved biking, planned to call her own baby Mark if it was a boy. If it was a girl, she liked the name Emma. The last time Fiona's mother saw her, on Thursday, 22 August, she was excited, buying clothes for the child, and a pair of shoes for herself to wear after her pregnancy when her feet were less swollen. She got wipes, Sudocrem – the baby was becoming a reality now, with less than two months to go. She was happy. Her mother and younger brother John, then just thirteen, left her at the door of the flat she shared with her boyfriend, John Thompson, in Church Street, Tullamore, a town right in the middle of Ireland. It's famous for its whiskey, and forms one point of the triangle in which these women disappeared. Although this is nowhere near the border, religion and politics still played a role in how Fiona's disappearance was perceived.

Fiona's mother said she was in good spirits when they left her, around 7 p.m. that evening. Her boyfriend was not home yet. As it was harvest season, he'd been working very long hours at his family's farm nine miles away; 350 acres of land that had made them well off for the area. According to John Thompson, Fiona was fine that night when he came home. When he left at six in the morning to go back to the farm, she was sitting up in bed. At 1 p.m. on that day, the Friday, her mother called around to the flat, but there was no answer at the door. She went back a few times over the following days, but there was no reply. It wasn't until the Saturday night that her mother and boyfriend spoke to each other and realised she was gone – each had apparently thought she was with the other. Because of this confusion, it was a full three days before the police started looking for Fiona. There were a lot of places to put a body round that area – a turf-cutting site with ponds, lakes, a river, a canal and reservoir. Bog land all around. Her family even went out to where her brother Mark's bike had been buried in the mountains, in case she had gone there, as she sometimes did when she was unhappy or wanted to feel close to him. Nothing. Months went by without a trace. The day her baby was due – 22 October – came and went, agonising for her family. As with many of the other cases, there were erroneous sightings and date mix-ups: someone claimed to have seen her in the shops on the Friday, but it turned out to be Thursday. Someone else said he'd seen her in London, but it was another woman from the area, who'd also just had a baby and had blonde hair.

In the press reports from the time, I was surprised to see so much weight given to the fact that Fiona and John were from different sides of the religious divide in Ireland. They lived in Southern Ireland, yet much of the news coverage of her case focuses on the fact that she was Catholic, like the majority in the country, and he was a wealthy landowning Protestant – a prejudice that's perhaps a hangover from famine times, when it was perceived that the landowners let people starve in the fields. The story is told as if they're Romeo and Juliet, in love across religious and class lines. I hadn't realised that sectarianism was so potent in the South as well. Fiona and John's families said it didn't bother them at all. Could religion really have been such a flashpoint in Ireland in 1996, not even in Northern Ireland?

In her pictures, Fiona Pender is strikingly glamorous, blonde and lipsticked, with a look of Madonna in *Evita*, a film released that same year. She worked as a hairdresser and did some modelling. She'd painted her motorbike pink, and her biking friends nicknamed her 'Barbie', a detail newspaper articles dwell on to a bizarre degree. Like Annie McCarrick, they describe her as stunning, striking, pretty, glamorous. A doomed blonde, like Princess Diana, who would die the following year. Fiona's case has had a lot of coverage, and part of this seems to be due to her beauty, her photogenic face, the tragedy of her unborn child. Some of her work involved modelling wedding dresses, though she would never be married herself, and those pictures were used too. Despite all the publicity, her case remains unsolved, and the beautiful blonde woman, the mother-to-be, has just vanished. So what happened to her? Only the clothes she was wearing and a handbag were missing. Did she really go to sleep safe, wake up, then leave the house, planning to see her mother a few hours later? Where would she have gone? How could she have disappeared so entirely, from a flat in the middle of a busy town?

◆ ◆ ◆

It's difficult to talk about Fiona Pender's case. So much is known yet not known, alluded to in hints and pseudonyms, but you get the sense that everyone, police, her family and the surrounding community, has a very good idea what happened to her. There is a suspect whose name is known, easily found online. Another person who seemingly can't be touched. There's a lot I can't say about this case, because of libel laws, and for a long time I was puzzled by the convoluted way it's described in the media and in books, but I can say that John Thompson, Fiona's boyfriend, was a suspect early on. At twenty-three, John was two years younger than Fiona and, as we've seen, from a very different background, but he said he loved her, that they were happy. They'd gone to London for a few months after her brother died, working in a hotel in Croydon and looking for a fresh start, but found they couldn't afford it and came home. Rumours went around, all the same. They used to have drunken fights, and she had once punched him, people said. She had apparently told her young brother, in confidence, that at the start of her pregnancy John had strangled her till she passed out. They'd had a fight that last night in the flat, the gossip went. The landlord didn't allow children in the property, so they would have had to move soon; maybe that was a factor. Maybe the long hours he was working also caused a rift, leaving her alone and pregnant, not able to go drinking or biking with her old friends.

John Thompson has given several interviews over the years to face these allegations head-on, adamant that he loved Fiona, that he had nothing to do with her disappearance. He admits, 'We often fought. There's no law against arguments.' In the picture the press usually use of him, he's a large young man, scowling and angry-looking. But perhaps you would be. If he didn't have anything to do with it, then it's rough for him – not only did he lose his girlfriend, he lost his unborn child too, and he's been living under a cloud of suspicion ever since. In 1997, he and his father, plus his three sisters, were arrested and questioned over Fiona's disappearance. All were released without charge. He claims Gardaí told him, falsely, that Fiona's body had been found, that he was going down for her murder. He says they mocked him and his family, told him he wasn't the father of Fiona's baby. The Gardaí have rejected the criticisms. John Thompson reportedly got married to a local woman with a child in 2004. It was said he was going to write a book, to set the record straight, but this hasn't materialised.

Years after Fiona disappeared, in 2014, a woman in Canada went to the police with a disturbing story. She was married to one of the suspects in the case, and said she had woken up to find he had dressed her in make-up and tights, and was raping her. There were videos of it. She said she'd passed out several times in the past and had no memory of what had happened to her. She said her husband told her he'd killed his girlfriend in Ireland, and would do the same to her. That he wanted to get Canadian citizenship so he could avoid extradition back to Ireland. But when he went on trial for this assault, he was acquitted, the judge accepting his argument that the videos showed consensual sex. This woman was also pregnant at the time. Pregnancy is one of the most dangerous times for women, when domestic violence often begins or escalates.

Women's Aid Ireland estimates that one in seven Irish women has experienced serious abuse from a partner – in Northern Ireland it's one in four, with domestic violence currently at its highest since records began. In the UK generally, two women every week are killed by former or current partners. Domestic violence is not an issue we've left behind in the nineties.

In 2008, a small wooden cross was found in the mountains about half an hour from Tullamore. It was marked 'Fiona Pender. Buried here, August 22nd, 1996'. The Gardaí dug up the area, but found nothing. A cruel joke? Who would do such a thing? The Gardaí also used heat-seeking helicopters in the search for her, drained a local canal, sent divers into a river. Nothing. Over the years they have sometimes searched again, acting on tip-offs, raising hope only to dash it again. It's one of those stories that makes you wonder how much sorrow one family can bear. Fiona's father Sean took his own life in 2000, unable to bear the loss of two of his three children, not to mention a grandchild so close to birth. As I've discussed, suicide was shattering in Ireland at the time, and until quite recently you could not be buried in a graveyard if you died that way, but even so Josephine Pender said she couldn't blame her husband. He looked twenty years younger in death, she said, finally at peace. The not knowing had been too much for him. Or perhaps having a very good idea who had killed their daughter, and watching that person walk around, free. Sean was found by his surviving son John, then just seventeen, and who is now the only one of the family left. John recently made a film about Fiona, called *My Sister Fi*. He's in his thirties now, and has a young daughter. Fiona's mother Josephine, having fought so long, died in 2017. She was only sixty-eight. Fiona's own child would have been twenty-four now. And yet Fiona still hasn't been found, and no one has been convicted of her murder. Her mother had no body to bury, she who'd buried a child and a husband already. Before she died,

Josephine maintained that she knew who had killed her daughter and grandchild, and she even had a strong suspicion of where Fiona was buried. She also mentioned the searches carried out to find the Disappeared from the North, which had yielded so much success. Could they not have done something similar for her daughter?

Two years after Fiona's disappearance, in February 1998, yet another young woman would vanish from her home, and never be seen again. She was also called Fiona. Fiona Sinnott was just nineteen and, tragically, she left behind a young daughter, who was a month shy of her first birthday. Separated from the father of her child, Sean, Fiona lived with her baby in a cottage in Ballyhitt, in a rural part of County Wexford, an hour's drive from Enniskerry. She had previously been in a violent relationship, and had been hospitalised several times, kicked in the head, her jaw almost broken once, her legs bitten another time. In 1996 when she was just seventeen, she had been threatened with a knife by this then boyfriend. She never made any official complaints against this man, so there was nothing in the records. By all accounts, however, Fiona was now enjoying life, and looking forward to celebrating her child's first birthday. Her family describe her as bubbly, lively, mischievous even. She loved music and baking, and had plans to become a pastry chef. She had long dark hair, and in fact looked not unlike Ciara Breen, who went missing in 1997.

The night of her disappearance, Fiona was in a local pub with friends, while Sean's parents looked after her daughter, Emma. In one of the many parallels between their cases, Emma was also the name Fiona Pender might have called her own child if it was a girl. Despite complaining of a pain in her arm and chest, she was reportedly in good form. At one point, she rang her brother Seamus from the pub to ask him to join her. Tired from his work as a fisherman, he declined – and would be left to wonder whether there was a subtext to her call, if someone was there who frightened Fiona, if she was trying to send him a message that he didn't understand or what might have happened if he'd said yes. Later, Fiona's ex, Sean, who had come in alone for a drink, apparently walked her home from the pub, ringing his mother to say Fiona wasn't feeling well, so he would spend the night with her. He asked his mother to pick him up and give him a lift in the morning. Fiona took two packets of peanuts with her from the pub, and the two moved off down the lane, into the dark. There were some reports of people hearing screams later on, as in many of these cases, but no one seems to have gone to investigate. Is screaming so common in rural Ireland that none of these apparent witnesses intervened?

According to Sean, he slept on the sofa in Fiona's house. Fiona had resolved to visit the doctor for her chest and arm pain, and he gave her some money for the bus. About five punts, around three British pounds, which wouldn't buy you much even in the nineties. His mother came to pick him up, and he left around nine in the morning. Fiona never made it to the doctor, and no one has seen her since. As Fiona didn't live with her parents, and had friends in different parts of the country and even England, it was a while before her family started to worry. Nine days later, the Gardaí would receive a report that Fiona had not been seen since the night she was at the pub. She hadn't come to collect her baby, she hadn't contacted any of her family, and Sean's parents, who still had her daughter, had apparently not found this strange enough to report it. When the police arrived at her house, they found it startlingly clean, emptied of possessions. As Fiona was not known for being house-proud, this was unusual. Alarm bells began to ring.

It would be very easy to hide a body in the area round Fiona's home. Not only is it rural, with miles of empty, boggy land, but there are several large lakes nearby, including Our Lady's Island Lake, which describes itself as the 'oldest Marian shrine' in Ireland. Marian means to do with the Virgin Mary, who has something of a cult following in Ireland and has even reportedly appeared there once or twice. It's the site of a pilgrimage every year and it's thought that it was used by female druids in pre-Christian times. A strange feature of the Irish countryside is it's dotted with places like this, holy wells and shrines and statues. They can be quite unnerving to come across in lonely spots, baby clothes and photos of the dead tied around them, lurid pictures of Jesus with his chest gaping open and hands bleeding.

As well as the bogs and lakes, the sea is only four miles away. From the nearby ferry port of Rosslare, it's possible to sail to the UK, or even France, and it wasn't uncommon for long-distance lorry drivers to spend the night camped nearby. In fact, a few months before she disappeared, Fiona had spent the night with a Welsh driver in the cab of his truck. The man was traced and revealed that while he was with her, someone had come knocking on the truck, angrily demanding that Fiona come out. It was her violent ex-boyfriend, the one who had pulled a knife on her. The driver said that Fiona seemed terrified of him. Again, because of the cautious way the case must be spoken of, it took me a while to figure out the identity of this man who came to find her.

Although more than a week had gone by before she was reported missing by her family, Gardaí searched hard for Fiona, even draining one of the small nearby lakes. They also searched the land of a local family, and dug up a septic tank. Nothing was found. Did she set off to see the doctor, and meet with some accident on the way? Did someone take her off the road, pulling her into a car – a favoured method of several of the suspects in the vanishing triangle cases? Was the pain in her arm something serious, that led to her death in some lonely spot, where her body has somehow never been found? Or did something happen in the house that night? Police thought that might have been the case, which would explain the suspiciously clean state of the house, and that whoever had caused her death had help to cover it up and move her body. They could never prove anything, however. What we do know is that, during the initial investigation into Fiona's disappearance, a local farmer called in to say some bags had been dumped on his land months before, around the time Fiona went missing. These bags had contained items of clothing and toys, and letters and documents with Fiona Sinnott's name on them. As if someone had cleared out her house and ditched her possessions, perhaps to make it look like she'd run away, leaving her baby behind. For some reason, the farmer had not contacted police at the time, and had destroyed the bags.

In both these cases, Fiona Pender and Fiona Sinnott, silence is a huge factor. People who know things but can't or won't say. Someone finding a huge dump of evidence but destroying it and not even telling the Gardaí until it was too late. It says a lot about Ireland that someone would come across a trove like this, and not make the connection to the missing woman, or else make it and still decide not to get involved. If you think of the priest digging up that body in 1996 in Northern Ireland, and telling no one, it's not so far-fetched that people would just sit on information. Then again, this was before the spread of the internet and of rolling news. The farmer may not have known about Fiona's case. Or it might have been another classic Irish case of keeping yourself to yourself, even if you find the belongings of a missing woman, even if you hear screams in the night, even if you see a distraught barefoot girl being pulled into a car by her hair, as witnesses apparently did on the night Jo Jo Dullard went missing.

Fiona Sinnott was another case of a young woman who some might have thought had 'gone astray'. The youngest of a loving family of five children, she'd begun to have relationships with men from the age of fifteen, and was pregnant without being married at eighteen. In some parts of Ireland in the nineties, this would have been seen as something shameful, especially if not followed by a shotgun wedding. Certainly at the time Gardaí thought she might have gone to England, or followed her lorry driver one-night stand, or been in a relationship with a married man. Did this obscure the obvious suspect in the case, who had a history of hurting her? I'm being careful in not naming this person, but it's another of those things that everyone knows and no one can say publicly.

In 2005, several people were arrested in connection with Fiona's case, but no charges were brought. In 2006 Gardaí dug up a field near Ballyhitt, after a tip-off, but they found nothing. Fiona's father was just fifty-nine when he died, and the family feel it was of a broken heart. Emma, Fiona's daughter, will be in her twenties now. She was brought up by her father's family, rarely seeing the Sinnotts except for an hour every two weeks at a local hotel. She won't remember anything of the mother who vanished before her first birthday, her life most likely taken by someone she knew, and had loved at one point, rather than by an unseen killer who prowled the roads of Ireland, looking for prey. It's not such a good story, is it, a woman killed by someone she knew and had let into the house, or even someone she lived with? Not a monster snatching her from a dark road, or out of her bedroom window, or from the car park of a pub, but an ordinary man. The truth is that the men who do these things, the monsters, are the same men who live in our homes. Larry Murphy, the rapist from the start of the book, had two kids, as did Mark Hennessy, Jastine Valdez's murderer, the youngest only a baby. David Lawler went home from killing and raping Marilyn Rynn and got into bed with his wife, took his child to school in the morning, got his wife pregnant again even after he was charged with murder. We tell young girls to look out for the stranger on the way home, hiding in the bushes or slowing down their car to offer you a lift, or, when you're younger, sweets or a stroke of a puppy. We don't tell them how to avoid getting into relationships with men who will break their bones and bite their flesh, leave them too terrified to escape. But sadly, and despite the fact that some of the women in this book were most likely abducted by a stranger, that's still where the greatest risk lies. Not on the road in the dark of night, but in your own home.

In a strange coda to the story – again, much like the finding of the cross with Fiona Pender's name on it – the Sinnotts put up a plaque to remember Fiona, on what would have been her thirtieth birthday, in 2008 (this was actually the same year the mysterious cross with Fiona Pender's name appeared). But before the plaque could be unveiled, they realised someone had prised it off the wall in the night and taken it away. It was replaced, and the same thing happened again. You have to wonder who would do this, and why. The parallels with Fiona Pender's case are remarkable. Again, the woman was last seen by the father of her child, at home apparently safe and well. Again, the man she was involved with was from a wealthier family, landowners. Again there was a child involved. And again the woman apparently vanished from her own home, with no trace of her ever to be found. There is no cautionary tale we can take from this case. No hitch-hiking at night, no sneaking out, no walking by herself in the countryside as darkness fell. Just falling in love, getting pregnant and being at home, and still she was gone.

As I dug further into these cases, I kept finding more names, even after more than a year of research. More dead or missing women in the same triangle area. Does that mean the disappearances didn't actually stop in 1998, as the accepted narrative goes? For example, Claire Boylan was thirty-six when she went missing from Terenure – about a mile from where Eva Brennan also went missing ten years before – in 2003. She was supposedly on her way to visit a friend in Tullamore, the same town where Fiona Pender went missing. The friend didn't know about the planned trip, and it's thought perhaps Claire didn't make it in the end. In her picture, Claire has a look of Eva too – short brown hair, and almost the same age. She worked in a bookshop. Like Eva, she was quiet and kept to herself, and she was also from a large family, of six children this time. She went missing from her home on a Sunday, also like Eva, and although Claire was known to have dropped out of her life sometimes for a few days, this time she hadn't taken a passport or any belongings, and her bank account has not been touched since she disappeared. There seems to be no recent progress on this case and very little publicity, although there is some discussion online about a possible suspect. Gardaí statements make clear that they thought that Claire had killed herself, and her case, like Eva's, also seems to have been largely forgotten, apparently never linked to the earlier disappearances. Was her case also clouded by her mental health issues and maybe her age? Should it have been linked to the other disappearances? Or is it simply that women go missing more often than we think?

There were Monica Riordan and Esra Uryn, two women in their thirties who separately went missing in 2011, also in Dublin. A coroner ruled that Monica, who was thirty-nine and known to struggle with alcohol and mental health issues, might have gone into the Liffey River. I note that she too went missing around Christmas – 20 December. Esra, whose car was found in Bray, County Wicklow, was thirty-four and had one child. She was English, of Turkish heritage. Her sister has since wondered if Mark Hennessy, the killer of Jastine Valdez, might have attacked Esra as well, since he lived very near Bray, and it's hard to believe Jastine was the first woman he'd ever hurt. Another possible suspect is Graham Dwyer, who murdered Elaine O'Hara the same year Esra went missing. Esra had only gone out in the morning to buy a pint of milk and she was never seen again. It strikes me how quickly the names slip from public record.

If they aren't well known enough to have a Wikipedia page – and the vanishing triangle women have to share one as it is – then there's little information about them. Is there not some way of keeping these names alive? Time has passed, yes, but the women have still not been found. We still don't know what happened to them. There are many others too, too many to list. In fact, there are lots of other women missing in Ireland, their families wondering where they are, not just the eight I originally began to look into. And there are lots of murders of women by men.

There was a man called Michael Bambrick at large during the time of the disappearances. He had killed his wife, Patricia, in 1991, and a woman named Mary Cummins in 1992, dismembering them both. When Annie McCarrick went missing in 1993, both of these women were just considered missing too, and Bambrick hadn't yet been charged, so he was free until 1995 and even allowed to take care of his two young daughters. Gardaí strongly suspected he had killed his wife and also Mary, whom he'd met in a pub, but they could find no evidence. He was only charged when he eventually confessed to the murders, and he got out of prison after thirteen years. I noticed that an article about Mary from the time used the headline 'unmarried' about her. She had a child, so this was probably meant pointedly. Just that one word, *unmarried*, as an epitaph for a whole life. As we've seen, Ireland was not kind to women who stepped out of line. The women Bambrick killed had three children between them, left motherless. He later said he'd killed his wife during rough sex, which she'd asked for – a precursor to the many cases we're now seeing where women are choked to death during sex.

Non-consensual BDSM is on the rise, and has been linked to the rise and availability of porn. As I was writing this book, a young British backpacker was murdered in New Zealand while on a Tinder date, and that man tried to use the same defence, ultimately unsuccessfully. He was not named, as is the law there, but she was, and her family and everyone else heard all about her final moments, how she'd died and how she lay dead in his room for a day, and were able to speculate about her sex life and sexual preferences. Her killer put her body in a suitcase and went on another date that same night. The use of this 'rough sex' or '*Fifty Shades of Grey*' defence has risen 90 per cent since 2010 in the UK – and since then at least fifty-nine women have been killed in this way. More often than not their killers get reduced sentences, just three years in some cases, as a result. The woman, dead and silenced, isn't around to say he's lying, or to defend herself. Too often it seems it's just an excuse for a more familiar phenomenon – violence against women. As I'm finishing the book, in July 2020, a bill to ban this defence is making its way through Parliament.

A quick glance over a list of murders in Ireland puts paid to the theory that it's a safe and welcoming country where bad things don't happen. There are a huge number of other stories I could tell – a report by Women's Aid Ireland, released in 2019, found that more than 200 women had been violently murdered in the country since 1996. That's an average of ten per year, which in a small country of less than 5 million is quite shocking. There's a huge interest in stories of serial killers, roaming psychopaths who prey on women. Of course they do exist, and there's a strong chance some of the triangle women were killed by such a person, but that's not the whole picture. It's not such an interesting story, but it is much more common for women to be murdered by the men they live with. Their partners, or even their fathers and sons. In three of the triangle cases, both Fionas and Ciara Breen, there are obvious suspects who've never been charged. Ciara was probably killed by a man she thought of as her boyfriend, and Fiona Sinnott had certainly been subjected to domestic violence in the past, as perhaps had Fiona Pender. This death toll of other women doesn't exactly bolster or crush the story of a potential serial killer, either caught for some other crime, or never caught and still out there. Instead, it shows something else about Ireland. That women are dying, and going missing, in disturbingly high numbers. That violence against women is pervasive in our society, and not going away.

Fiona Pender, as we've seen, went missing in 1996, heavily pregnant and vulnerable. Two other events took place that same year that I think are relevant to this story. One was in America, the trial of O.J. Simpson for the murder of Nicole Brown, his ex-wife, and a man named Ron Goldman, which gripped Ireland as much as everywhere else. I heard far more about this case than about any of the missing women on my own doorstep. Nicole was also a beautiful, doomed blonde. I remember taking in the fact that O.J. had been acquitted, despite what the prosecution had felt was overwhelming evidence against him: the victims' blood in his car; a bloody glove at his home that was the twin of one at the site; the fact he'd fled from police. Plus the multiple accusations that he'd beaten Nicole Brown savagely, the pictures of her bruised face, the recorded calls to 911 where she shouted that he was going to kill her. There was a potent message in this for young girls watching, as I was: even if it's obvious who hurt you, you still might not be believed. And once you're dead, there really is no one to speak for you. Reading up on the case now, I'm depressed to find that the prosecution barely mentioned the domestic violence angle in court, as they could see the jury didn't care. Even a juror who was later dismissed when it emerged she was a victim of domestic abuse herself, told the press that what Nicole had endured was 'a whole lot of nothing'. Although O.J. was acquitted, he was later found guilty in a civil trial and ordered to pay damages, something that also happened in Ireland after the Omagh bombers walked free in criminal court, largely due to a technicality about search warrants. There was no justice for Nicole Brown in the highest-profile trial of the decade, so it's hardly surprising there would be none for other women, ordinary women.

◆ ◆ ◆

Also in 1996, another woman was murdered in Ireland, in a horrific crime that remains unsolved. Again there is a chief suspect, and in all likelihood her murder is not linked to the others in the triangle – Cork is on the other side of the country – but since it took place during the same time I think it's relevant. It certainly touches on a lot of the themes in this book: judgement of the dead woman, speculation about her private life, silence and lies, a suspect who's never been convicted and police incompetence, where they simply botched the enquiry from the beginning. Sophie Toscan du Plantier was thirty-nine, a wealthy, sophisticated Parisian, a TV producer married to a successful film mogul, who'd fallen in love with the area of West Cork and often came to her holiday home there alone, leaving her husband and son in France. Two days before Christmas 1996 – again the Christmas connection – Sophie was found beaten to death at the side of the road, her head crushed with a concrete block, her limbs tangled painfully in barbed wire. That day, she had driven to Cork airport and tried to get a flight back to Paris but they were all full, so she planned to leave the next day instead – another of those painful 'what if' moments involving transport. At 10 p.m. she called her housekeeper and asked her to come at ten the next morning so she could close up the house, because she was going home for Christmas. Her son Pierre-Louis, then fifteen, was with his father for the holiday, and Sophie planned to spend it with her second husband, Daniel. She had already called her gardener and asked him to plant a tree for Daniel at their country home, as a Christmas gift. These were people who owned several homes around the world and moved in sophisticated circles. She had plans to fly on to Dakar for New Year, an example of the glamorous, high-profile life she led, so out of step with the rural peace she enjoyed in Cork. All of it would end that night, on a desolate lane in the very west of Ireland. She was in her nightclothes when she was found, her feet slipped into her walking boots. As if someone had come to the door and woken her from sleep. Someone, presumably, to whom she might have opened it. She was halfway down her drive, as if someone had chased her and she'd run, getting as far as her gate, putting her hands on it, then no further. There were only three houses on the lane, a small country one with a cattle grid, little more than a dirt track really. There was no sign of a break-in at the house, but when the housekeeper arrived the next day, she said she noticed right away that the poker was missing. Sophie had called her husband at 11 p.m., and that was the last time anyone spoke to her. Anyone but her killer, probably. There is some confusion over whether anyone nearby heard screams or not. They would have gone to her aid if so, surely, or called the Gardaí. Or perhaps not, as we've seen from other cases in this book.

A chief suspect quite quickly emerged. An English man named Ian Bailey, who lived locally, was seen to have scratches on his hands and face on Christmas Day – someone captured them on video when he attended the local sea swim, an event they also do in my village. He said they were from killing a turkey and chopping down a Christmas tree. Bailey talked about Sophie's murder a lot, people said. A journalist who lived close to her home, he had been one of the first on the scene, and had reported extensively on the case. He told everyone the police suspected him, almost as if he got a kick out of it. It soon emerged that Ian Bailey had attacked his current partner Jules twice in the past, once just months before Sophie's death, biting her and pulling out a clump of her hair. Later, in 2001, he would attack Jules again, hitting her with one of the crutches he'd been given after tearing his Achilles tendon. She would be hospitalised each time, with serious injuries. Sophie was found clutching hair in her clenched hand, that turned out to be her own, as if someone had pulled it from her head, as if she had fought back, which might have left scratches on her attacker. Other allegations piled up against Bailey. A local woman, Marie Farrell, made an anonymous call from a phone box to report that she saw Bailey near Sophie's house late on the night of the murder; this being Ireland, it was easy to work out who'd called. She didn't want to go public as she'd been driving in a car with another man, not her husband. Bailey actually admitted himself that he'd been out that night, but of course he lived very nearby. Like Sophie, Ian Bailey was a writer, a poet who gave loud performances of his work. He kept a diary too, and frequently roamed the countryside at night, claiming he did his best work then. He was said to howl at the moon, to be a bit of a weirdo. But that doesn't add up to murder. Yes, he had attacked his partner several times, and had scratches on him the day after Sophie was found. A neighbour said he'd made a bonfire at his house on Boxing Day, three days after the murder – he denied this. Various people made other allegations, that he'd told them or shown them incriminating things, but nothing was ever proved and he has always denied any involvement.

Sophie, like American Annie McCarrick, apparently felt safe in Ireland, although her husband had been worried about her buying a house in such an isolated spot, and going there alone for the first time. But she had been on holiday there many times before, although always with other people, and it was so quiet. Murders didn't happen in Ireland unless you were affected by the Troubles, miles away from the emptiness of rural Cork. It's no surprise she wouldn't have felt a sense of danger there. Sophie's life in West Cork was completely outside her normal world. She even went by her maiden name there, Bouniol. There were rumours in the press about what she did in the isolated house she'd bought, in this country she had no connection to. That she might get back together with her first husband, that she had a lover, a third man. That she and Daniel were fighting – certainly they had separated a few times before, but got back together. There were two used wine glasses in the house, and the chairs were arranged in an unusual way, two of them pulled out, although her family noted that she liked to sit that way, with her legs propped up, so perhaps it was nothing. A bottle of champagne sat unopened on a coffee table.

Sophie's husband Daniel was quite a bit older than her at fifty-five, a successful film producer whom she had met at the Cannes Film Festival. He was a high-profile man, a friend of Jacques Chirac, then President of France. It seemed they spent a lot of time apart, that Sophie was trying to establish an identity for herself outside her marriage. She used the isolated cottage to write: documentary scripts, diary entries. I wonder if she felt that her first marriage, having a child young, had dampened down her potential, and she was ready to start again when her life was brutally cut short. It strikes me that all the missing and dead women had plans – to become a mother, to train as a teacher, to meet an estranged father for the first time, or simply to have a quiet peaceful life. The future they'd planned was taken from them when their steps put them in the path of someone evil. However, the couple were happy together, Daniel said, they wanted to have a baby, which they'd call Thérèse if it was a girl. The Irish papers picked up on the fact Sophie had had two husbands. 'Twice-married Sophie', they called her, as if that had anything to do with it. 'Socialite' was another word used often, and I'm not even sure what that means. Rich? Flighty? There was a lot of talk too about how beautiful she was, as if that explained what happened to her.

Daniel died in 2003. Sophie's family, including her son, have repeatedly launched lawsuits against Ian Bailey and done their best to marshal the might of the French state against this rural corner of Ireland. 'A killer walks the hills,' they said. It hasn't worked. Their planned civil suit collapsed after a key witness, Marie Farrell, withdrew her statement, saying Gardaí had pressured her into it in an effort to frame Bailey. A few years later, Ian Bailey tried to sue the media for saying he was Sophie's killer, in a libel case that turned into something of a trial of his guilt. The judge threw out six of Bailey's eight claims, upholding his insistence that he'd never beaten his ex-wife, who lived in England and never commented on the case at all. The judge also described him as 'a violent man', and Bailey did not come out well from the trial on the whole, but there was simply no proof that he had done it. Police incompetence was once again a factor – they lost key evidence from Sophie's home, including a wine bottle found in undergrowth, and a bloodied gate, and failed to follow up witness sightings. How do you lose a whole gate? It was the first murder for decades in this area, and it was a savage one. Daniel, Sophie's husband, suggested that the Gardaí didn't want to harm tourism in the area by digging too deep, but surely a brutal unsolved murder would be worse than a solved one. Sophie's body was exhumed in 2004 to look for evidence, but before that she had already been re-buried once, in France. It's hard to imagine evidence surviving that, not to mention the twenty hours she lay on the ground, plus however long it was between her death and her body being found, at least eight hours.

Sophie's murder took place on the other side of the country from the vanishing triangle, and her body was not hidden or buried, but left on the road to be found the next day, Christmas Eve. It seems unlikely there's a connection to the other women who were hurt around this time. But on the other hand, Ireland is small, as we've said. Nothing can be discounted. Why did this case receive so much attention? The brutal nature of the crime, the injuries inflicted on a slight, fair woman, a sophisticated foreign woman? Why do we care so much about her and not about other women – Eva Brennan, say, who was the same age as Sophie, and whose disappearance was apparently not investigated for three months?

As with the triangle cases, it's likely we'll never know the truth until someone talks. But it's far from over. As I write this, it's just a few months since Ian Bailey was convicted 'in absentia' – that is, in his absence – by a French court, though he's always said he's innocent, and that he can explain the unfortunate circumstantial details that seemed to damn him. Maybe that's the hardest thing about these cases. To accept that we will just never know for sure.

What most of the cases in this chapter have in common is the fact that there is an obvious suspect, whose name is known to everyone locally, but who cannot be charged. Silence reigns, and the families have to suffer the pain of seeing the likely perpetrator walking free, living their lives. The only case I remember hearing about at the time, of any of these, was Sophie's. However, I was researching her death – a major news story that still makes headlines today – when I discovered another woman had been killed just six days after her, in Dublin. This woman, Belinda Pereira, was Sri Lankan, and a sex worker, and she was bludgeoned to death in an apartment she was renting. It's striking how little coverage her murder – also unsolved to this day – has had compared to Sophie's. There are hardly any news stories about it – I found only two – and no apparent movement on the case. Belinda was only in Ireland for the Christmas period, working out of a flat in Dublin. It's thought up to thirty men went there during those few weeks. Police think robbery was the motive, as several thousand pounds was stolen from her. She was only twenty-six when she died, a strikingly beautiful woman with a huge smile. Another two women were murdered that same year, one also a sex worker in Dublin, stabbed over what was thought to be a drugs debt, and one stabbed by a man she'd offered a lift to. It seems that even when women are the ones offering the lifts their lives are in danger. And that there's a hierarchy of death. If you are beautiful, blonde, a mother, a married woman, then people will care about your murder. If you aren't, you might be out of luck.

There was a final triangle case, the last disappearance, in 1998, that really got to me. Something about Deirdre Jacob's case chills me to the bone, even more than the others. Perhaps I identify with her the most – she was only two years older than me, and had moved to England to study, as I would in 2000. I found a picture of Deirdre in what looks like her home or university bedroom – a single bed, the walls Blu-Tacked with posters and eighteenth-birthday cards. She's smiling over her shoulder, in a denim shirt, pretty and happy. That could have been my room around the same time. There are no complicating factors in Deirdre's case. No violent man in her past, no secret older boyfriend, no hitch-hiking at night or walking about the countryside alone. She vanished from outside her own home in Newbridge, less than an hour from Dublin, in the middle of the day, a baffling and therefore terrifying case. How can this happen to someone, on a busy road, on a bright summer's day? I know very well what it was like to come back to Ireland for the summer. I know she would probably have thought herself safe. She would have been warned, be careful in London. We all knew murders happened there, girls dragged into the shadows or down alleys. We knew not to take lifts there. We knew not to talk to strangers. But not here, not in Ireland. It was safe here. Certainly it was safe to walk a few miles into town then back again, in the middle of the day in high summer. Or so she would have thought.

Deirdre was at teacher training college in Twickenham, London. Irish summers can seem long when you've been away somewhere with more life about it. I wonder how she might have felt that day. Itching to get back to the fun of studying in a big city, perhaps. Perhaps sad to be going away again soon, or for how you can never truly go home again once you've left, once you've changed yourself to fit into the person England needs you to be, modulated your accent and learned to smile at jokes about potatoes. Like the American woman, Annie McCarrick, five years earlier, Deirdre had gone to the bank the day she disappeared, to get a money order to pay her next year's fees at teacher training college. Also like Annie, she was captured on the CCTV there, another woman frozen in her last ever recorded image. The time was 14.35. A short while later, she walked past a security camera on the street with what looks like purpose, in a dark T-shirt and loose trousers, carrying a shoulder bag with the distinctive Caterpillar logo, a brand that was big in Ireland at the time. Her dark hair was bobbed. Like Imelda Keenan back in 1994, another woman who disappeared in the middle of the day, she went to the post office to send off her money. She dropped in to her grandmother's, who lived on the way. Then she walked back home, along the river and main road. At least eight people saw her on the way, up to a point where she was metres from her door, almost at the gate of her house. And then, somehow, Deirdre vanished. She didn't make it inside, and when her mother came home from work a few hours later, she wasn't there. No trace of her has ever been found. On the CCTV, I watched her make that doomed walk several times. Just seconds of footage. Something heavy lodged in my chest. What happened to her after this? Where did she go? Or perhaps what we should be asking is – who took her? It's hard to comprehend a pain like that, of a much-loved daughter simply vaporising. What could have happened to her so close to home? On a busy road, with neighbours and acquaintances passing? Where could she have gone?

One possibility is she was pulled into a car – a man drives up, winds down his window, asks for directions. You're a polite girl, well brought up, so you go over to help, and the man drags you into the car. As we'll see in some later cases, where luckily the girl managed to get away to tell the tale, this is by no means impossible or unheard of in Ireland. It's also very similar to the MO of Larry Murphy's crime, less than two years after Deirdre disappeared. Larry Murphy, in fact, once did some work for Deirdre's grandmother, who owned a local sweetshop, and when she died a few years later, a flyer with his name on it was found among her belongings. As part of his carpentry work he made wooden toys for children, a small but chilling detail. Naturally, this seemed like an important clue, Deirdre linked to a man who by then was known to pull women into cars and abduct them. But it's circumstantial evidence at best and the Gardaí were never able to prove a link.

In many of these cases, we've seen the impact of false information and sightings, either through malice, fear, or just getting the dates wrong in a well-meaning attempt to help. In Deirdre's case, a man called the police and media several times, claiming he'd given her a lift that day. This wasted a lot of time, and gave her parents false hope that she might have gone to visit friends, as she had the weekend before she went missing. Eventually the man was tracked down – it turned out his own daughter had died in a car accident and he was unhinged by it. There were no further leads. Deirdre went missing on 28 July 1998 and hasn't been seen since. In 2018, twenty years on, her case was declared a murder, and the police said they were looking into Larry Murphy again as a suspect, although so far nothing has come of it. Retired Garda Pat Marry felt this was the right line of enquiry, and that perhaps Murphy might have confessed if pressed more while he was in prison. Of all the cases, only Deirdre's and Fiona Pender's have this status as murders. The rest are still simply missing.

I asked Alan Bailey and Pat Marry, the retired detectives I spoke to, for their views on the case, and it seems widely accepted that Deirdre's disappearance is linked to that of some of the other women. For example, she went missing very close to where Jo Jo Dullard was last seen almost three years before – only fifteen miles, and both from main roads. Could someone have driven up, grabbed her and been gone before anyone could see? Think of the lightning-quick attack, the abduction and rape executed by Larry Murphy just two years after Deirdre's disappearance, or the speed with which Mark Hennessy took Jastine Valdez twenty years later, in 2018, pulling her into a car so fast that her phone and groceries were abandoned on the side of the road, and witnesses could do nothing to stop it. It's possible. After Deirdre, there would be no more such disappearances in the triangle for some time. If the same person was responsible for them all, why did they stop? Could it be that this person was caught not long after for another crime, in prison and unable to kill any more?

By 1998, five years had gone by since Annie McCarrick went for a walk on a March afternoon and never came back. Since then, seven more women had gone missing, and several more been murdered, all in the same area. Something was going on, but Gardaí could do nothing. There had been no charges, no confirmed suspects, no trials. Even in cases where a body was found, as with Sophie Toscan du Plantier and Marie Kilmartin, there was no resolution. We don't even know if the dates are right. People who catalogue the vanishing triangle cases often consider Deirdre Jacob to have been the last victim, but that may not have been the case – certainly there were murders and disappearances afterwards. Scratch the surface of any year, and you'll find women who are missing or killed, and still no one knows what happened to them. Violence against women, both from men they know and from strangers, is sadly commonplace in Ireland. So what were the Gardaí going to do about it?

Chapter Eight

The Police

Once I looked under the surface, I began to see the nuances behind this serial killer narrative. It's too simplistic, and it overlooks the fact that violence against women was much more common than I'd ever thought, as a girl in Ireland. Instead of a single serial killer abducting all eight women, it's likely that at least three of them were killed by men they knew, suspects who were very much on the police radar, but who nonetheless were never charged or convicted. And of course the most egregious example in the book, that of Arlene Arkinson, who was last seen with a man already known to target young girls, who still walked free to do it again. Why was this allowed to happen?

I talked earlier about the failures of different institutions – the Church, the state and even the terrorist organisations. Then there was the police – two different forces on one small island, both of them failing in different ways. I asked Garda Pat Marry why it happened so often that the obvious suspects were not charged. Was it simply time and budget – could the police have done more? Or was it that there's little to be done in a case with no body and no forensic evidence? It's one thing to know that someone is guilty, and quite another to prove it in court. Pat said that of course they could have done more, it's always possible. A lot depends on the individual officer, how tenacious they are that particular day, how attuned to tiny lies and evasions, how willing to follow up multiple leads that might be wild goose chases, and how much support they get from their higher-ups. He mentioned several cases where he had to fight to get the budget to follow up a lead that eventually unravelled the whole case – you can read more on this in his book, *The Making of a Detective*. He felt that Operation Trace, the cold-case review of the triangle cases, could have done even more, pressed harder on certain suspects, followed up on witnesses sooner and more thoroughly. Having worked on Ciara Breen's case himself, he had seen how mistakes let that case go unsolved. He said that most Gardaí at the time were simply not equipped or experienced enough to deal with this kind of sexual murder, and in some cases were too concerned with what the press thought; the PR of a case.

I'm trying not to be unfair to the Gardaí here. I know the Troubles put a huge strain on the police, even in the South, and that they weren't trained to handle this kind of murder, the non-sectarian kind. As we saw in the cases of Annie and Eva, they could barely entertain the idea that a man would abduct a woman he didn't know and kill her. Nor did they have any expertise in handling missing persons cases, something that is still lacking in Ireland. There was no database of crimes, no way to link past incidents; for example to find a man who'd tried to abduct a woman before but she'd managed to escape, or who had raped or hurt or imprisoned someone, all the warnings signs that are almost always there if you look.

This lack of expertise or central coordination is partly why it took so long to link the different cases – they were usually handled by officers in the local Gardaí station, who might not have had any experience with murders or even missing people. In some cases, as we've seen, they made assumptions – such as that the woman had killed herself. That she'd gone off with a man, or been depressed because of an abortion. Who's to know what damage these assumptions did, in missing early clues during the crucial first days after someone has gone? There are many accusations of the police failing to take a case seriously, not doing enough, not acting sooner. Targeting the grieving family instead of the obvious suspect, as the RUC did with Arlene's case. Interviewing witnesses with the suspect in the room, as they did with Vincent Connell and his girlfriend. Failing to start the search soon enough, or giving up too easily. It's true as well that the police didn't have the budget or time to follow up every single tiny clue or hint, and that in some cases they were fighting against a wall of lies and silence. All the same, it must be gutting for the families to know that a little bit more work might have sent their daughter's killer to jail, or at least let them have her body back to bury.

As we've seen, in some of these cases the police and everyone locally know the identity of a chief suspect, and the name is readily found online, but no one can say it officially because that person has never been convicted. In small Irish towns, family members might see this man around the place, filling up their car or buying groceries. Sadly, this is a situation familiar to many other families in Ireland, whose loved ones were killed in terror attacks. A name spoken in private, a growing whisper, never to appear in print or, it seems, on a charge sheet. Another one of the ghost men in this story. So why can't these people be arrested? I don't know what's worse – not having any idea what happened to your daughter, or knowing exactly what did, and having to see the man who hurt her walking around every day in complete freedom.

This same situation arose in the summer of 1998: to the families of those killed in the Omagh bombing, who also knew the people who'd killed their loved ones and had to watch them go free. That year was the end of the Troubles in Northern Ireland, when nonetheless fifty-four people died, over half of these in Omagh on a Saturday in August, the last, worst atrocity in decades of atrocities. I don't think I'll ever forget that morning, watching it unfold, death after death, and no reason to it, Catholics as well as Protestants, visitors from other countries, children and teenagers, babies. It was cruel in so many ways, partly the huge loss of life – at twenty-nine the largest single attack in the Troubles – and partly the spread of the victims, from unborn children to girls my age, everyone you might find on a busy high street in a market town on a Saturday. The car bomb was placed to do maximum damage, and the warning phoned in only made things worse – they said the wrong place, and so the police unwittingly herded people, instead of to safety, right into the blast zone. It was also cruel because we thought by then it was over – we'd waited, tense, as the Good Friday Agreement was brokered in April that year, truly believing it was the end. Then in July, Loyalist terrorists fire-bombed a Catholic home, killing three young brothers, aged seven, eight and nine. No one was caught for it, although locally names were mentioned. That was bad enough. Then Omagh. I remember going to a memorial service later in the summer, something that had never been held before during all the Troubles that I could recall, and was happening all over the North that day. That was how bad people felt about it, what a terrible shocking summer it had been. We were almost punch-drunk from it, desperate for it to end.

Although the bomb attack took place in Northern Ireland (not far from where Arlene Arkinson lived, in fact), the people who made and planted the bomb lived on the other side of the border. Everyone knew who did it – exactly like in Arlene's case – they just couldn't prove it, and again the case was bungled, a small matter of an invalid search warrant allowing the guilty to walk free. One person was convicted in 2002, but was released on appeal three years later. Over the years there have been more charges and even criminal trials, which have all failed, one as recently as 2016.

However, Omagh was different. It was a watershed in so many ways: we would not live like this anymore, not when peace had been so close. The families refused to accept that no one would be prosecuted, to go away quietly in the name of peace. When the criminal trial fell apart, they brought a civil case against one of the bombers, and won. It might not have amounted to much but it was a landmark case all the same. The family of Sophie Toscan du Plantier have similarly tried several times to extradite Ian Bailey to France to stand trial, since he's never been charged in Ireland, but with no success. In 2019 he was convicted of murder in absentia, as we've seen. The families of Nicole Brown and Ron Goldman also brought a civil case against O.J. Simpson in 1996, and won substantial damages. It's so strange that this can happen; that civil cases can be won against someone who has been found not guilty in a criminal court. It seems a tacit admission that being cleared in a criminal court doesn't mean you are innocent. It just means that, by the standards we've set for ourselves as a society, we can't show sufficient proof. The RUC was officially criticised for its conduct of the Omagh investigation, the way it mishandled evidence and failed to follow up leads, thus allowing mass murderers to go free. The force was by then on its last legs in any case, and would not survive much longer.

◆　◆　◆

It's clear that the RUC was more than capable of bungling cases. What about the Gardaí – did they also make fatal mistakes? I met

Alan Bailey on a miserable rainy June day in Dublin in June 2019. Alan was a detective on Operation Trace, the Gardaí task force into the triangle cases, set up when someone finally looked at all these missing women and wondered if maybe there was a connection. Garda Commissioner Pat Byrne set up the force in late 1998, a year in which another two women had gone missing. There were to be six Gardaí on the team, including two women, and a superintendent. Many of them had worked on related cases, such as the murder of Antoinette Smith, who was killed and buried in the triangle back in 1987. Hopes were high that this was the best possible way to solve the mystery of all the missing women. From the start, however, there was hostility to the cold-case team. Although the Gardaí who worked on the initial cases tried hard to look for most of these women, it's clear they were still stuck in the old ways of doing things, which led to some wildly inadequate responses as we've seen, with searches not being started for days or even weeks. Nor were they used to being called out on their actions, so the idea of someone double-checking their work wasn't all that popular.

Operation Trace only looked at six of the women – not Imelda Keenan, missing from Waterford city centre in 1994, and not Eva Brennan, who left her family home after a row in 1993. Just Fiona Sinnott, Ciara, Deirdre, Annie, Jo Jo and Fiona Pender. The detectives were told by higher-ups what cases to focus on, and not given a choice, and they didn't know why. Geography, perhaps, since Imelda lived further away from Dublin, or the lingering conviction that Eva had killed herself. Each detective would take one case, look at it in detail, and then swap, the idea being that fresh eyes would maybe see that one tiny clue that could unravel the whole picture. They pinned the women's photos to the wall to remind them what they were doing. When they began, the phrase *serial killer* was of course in their minds, but they resolved to assume nothing. And remember, there was no proof of anything, barely any evidence at all. They didn't know if they were looking for the same killer, or six different ones. Although there had been brutal killers in Ireland, there had never before been a hunt for a serial predator, someone who stalked victims on lonely roads and pulled them into cars; abducted complete strangers. Would they find one right under their noses?

Alan worked full time on these cases for three years. He went to England to learn about the HOLMES case database (Home Office Large Major Enquiry System) and to Canada, which had a system called ViCAP (which stands for Violent Criminal Apprehension Program) that also linked in sexual assaults, acknowledging that perpetrators often work their way up to murder. Nothing like these databases existed in Ireland at the time, and of course there was no DNA registry since it was such a new technology, although with the David Lawler arrest (in 1995), they were beginning to see the possibilities of that method of detection. The Phyllis Murphy case, twenty years old, was broken within a year of Trace being set up, and although it was not part of their remit, they knew there was a chance that it was connected, and it must have given them a much-needed boost of hope when her killer was finally caught, again from DNA evidence. Operation Trace set up an anonymous tip-line, which brought in almost 8,000 leads. Names to be looked at. Rumours. Stories. Everything from someone who'd once stolen underwear off a washing line, to flashers and people who just seemed dodgy. The officers had computers, still quite new to the force, which many of them had to learn to use for the first time. Eventually, they designed their own database system, which would also include violent sexual assaults, to be called OVID (which stands for Offender, Victim, Incident Database). They learned about victimology, offender signatures, geographic profiling.

Alan Bailey has written an in-depth book about this himself, called *Missing, Presumed*. In it he tells an ironic story that illustrates what they were working against, the bureaucracy and stonewalling, the hostility to modernisation. A request had been put in for six filing cabinets, so they could catalogue all the evidence in each case. When they turned up, they were already full of top-secret evidence from other cases, pertaining to intelligence and national security – no one had picked up on the fact they needed to be *empty* filing cabinets, and the man who delivered them wouldn't take them away again, since his job was only to bring them. Alan has devoted his working life to helping people, and in his retirement works in a day centre for homeless people in central Dublin. He talked in great detail about the cases, every fact recalled with an ease that showed me he's thought about these women a lot. He didn't forget. Clearly, the fact that the operation didn't find any of them weighs on his mind.

Operation Trace ran for three years. During that time, there were moments of hope. They looked at David Lawler, in prison since 1996 for killing Marilyn Rynn the year before. When Larry Murphy surfaced in 2000, an apparently practised abductor who'd been in front of their noses the whole time, undetected, that seemed like a major breakthrough. He was going to kill his victim in Carlow, surely, and it seemed so unlikely it was a first attempt. But when questioned, he quite politely declined to say anything. And how could they make him? There were no bodies. A few bits of circumstantial evidence that maybe showed his path had crossed with those of some of the women, hardly unusual in a place like Ireland. Then there was John Crerar, the obvious suspect who'd somehow got away with a brutal killing for twenty years. What were the chances he murdered one woman in 1979, then never again? Wasn't it more likely that he'd been sloppy the first time, leaving her body where it could be found, her possessions scattered about her? He'd have been caught then if DNA testing had existed. Perhaps if Crerar killed again, he covered his tracks more thoroughly.

The pathology of such men is well documented, that they often begin as small children with cruelty to animals or perhaps sexual assaults on other kids, and then they graduate to assaulting women, rape, sometimes associated with house break-ins or robbery (Robert Howard's exact MO and progression). This was seen in America with notorious serial killer Ted Bundy, and with the Golden State Killer, who as of June 2020, when he confessed, we know is a man named Joseph James DeAngelo, now aged seventy-four. It took the police in California years to realise that the serial rapist they'd had on their books since the seventies had morphed into the prolific murderer they were now hunting. After a while his crimes stopped, which conventional wisdom suggests only happens if a killer dies, or goes to prison, or there's some notable event like he gets married. We don't yet know what caused the cessation in the Golden State Killer's activity, when he had already raped and killed staggering numbers of people.

The Irish disappearances and murders of the nineties and before are thought to have ended in 1998, although as I've listed in the chapter above, there were several other later incidences of both that could possibly be connected. Both Murphy and Crerar were in prison by 2002, which could explain why the crimes stopped then (it took three years between arrest and conviction for Crerar, which shocks me a little but seems normal in Ireland). Or perhaps a killer might have been spooked, for a few years anyway, by the rise of DNA testing. Who knows?

I asked Alan Bailey about Arlene Arkinson's case, and he winced. They had of course been aware of it, and come to the same conclusion as me, that a potential killer wouldn't be deterred by a border, especially one that was just a line on a map, and that Howard had very likely killed Arlene and possibly other women. Alan had attended Robert Howard's trial along with some colleagues, and he spoke of his frustration that the jury weren't allowed to be told of his many previous convictions for rape, or that he was currently in prison for murdering a girl a year younger than Arlene. Although Howard went back to prison after the trial, the innocent verdict was still clearly devastating for the detectives, especially as had he gone on trial in Ireland, the jury would have been told the full story. It means another case is technically unsolved, with no leverage to try to find Arlene's body, and of course Howard is dead now anyway, the truth gone with him.

Then there was a very bizarre lead, when a Canadian serial killer claimed he had travelled to Ireland in the nineties with another man, and that they had killed the missing women. He said he knew exactly where five of the Irish women were buried, and could take Gardaí there if he was allowed out of prison to travel to the country, something that was never going to happen. Besides, Clifford Robert Olson was known for targeting children, not women, and psychologically that's a very different MO. All the same, Alan spoke to him several times on the phone, negotiating for the evidence Olson supposedly had, but it was another dead end. It seems he hoped that a trip to Ireland might perhaps allow him to escape life in prison. It's surprisingly common for convicted killers to give false confessions to other crimes.

Several other serving prisoners at the time gave tip-offs to Operation Trace, and the detectives followed up on these, but nothing was ever found. Perhaps these people just wanted the attention, the drama of being involved in an investigation, or the twisted glory of claiming responsibility for something they knew nothing about. Or maybe they really did know something and actually wanted to help, but, as we've seen from the ICLVR searches, it's hard to remember the exact location of a body after thirty years. After all, the killers back then were trying to hide the bodies so that they wouldn't ever be found.

This being Ireland, there were also quite a few calls from self-proclaimed psychics and visionaries. It's a fact they don't like to advertise, but the Gardaí are not above using psychics on occasion. Whatever the truth, nothing came of these tips either.

In 2008 a minister in the Irish government, John McGuinness TD, went so far as to say the Gardaí had bungled the cases of the missing triangle women, branding it a 'national disgrace'. The Gardaí had refused to modernise, he said, to take advantage of technology, and they hadn't acted fast enough on many of the cases. To be fair to the Gardaí, they have looked hard for all the women since – and, as they point out, with no bodies or crime scenes, there's only so much they can do, unless people talk.

In the case of Sophie Toscan du Plantier, which attracted accusations of Gardaí incompetence, there was some DNA recovered from the scene, but not enough to get a full profile, and a review in 2002 found no fault in the investigation into her murder. But certainly evidence was lost, foot impressions wiped out at the scene. It was twenty hours before they could get a pathologist out to check the body, because there was only one for the whole country and it was almost Christmas, and so Sophie lay there all day, on that freezing lane, barren fields of moss and heather on either side. Someone had covered her with a blue sheet or tarpaulin. In 2014 another scandal hit Ireland when it emerged that Gardaí stations, including the one handling Sophie's case, had been unlawfully recording phone calls in and out, perhaps even ones between solicitors and clients. There was a sense that, in these rural areas, the Gardaí were a bluff, insular group of men, sometimes with other jobs on the side like farming, who knew everyone and handled cases according to their personal allegiances and prejudices. In the missing persons cases, the Gardaí were hampered by lack of evidence, and perhaps by not taking action soon enough. And of course we know they made mistakes in other cases, so the same could have happened in the triangle ones. Here's one example.

In 1997 there were a couple of other murders in the triangle that I haven't mentioned yet, which became known as the Grangegorman killings. Two women who were in-patients at a psychiatric hospital were stabbed many times, mutilated so badly that it was described at the time as the worst crime in Ireland. In that case, the wrong man was convicted at first due to some undeniable Gardaí bungling, and the guilty one didn't go on trial until 2015. Dean Lyons, a man with learning difficulties and a heroin addiction, had confessed to the murders early on, but kept changing his story, and didn't even know key details of the crime. Meanwhile, Mark Nash, the real killer, had also confessed to the murders while under arrest for another double homicide the same year, 1997. Unlike Dean Lyons, he knew details that hadn't been released. Somehow the information that Dean was innocent didn't get passed on for months. Nash was at least already in prison, and Dean Lyons was cleared and released, but not before spending nine months in prison for something he didn't do. He would die in 2000 of an overdose.

It just goes to show how easily mistakes are made, and how slow the police can be to fix them. Nash was twenty-five when he murdered four people in a matter of months – had he perhaps done it before? He'd have been twenty-one when Annie went missing. It's very possible that something like this had happened before; that someone innocent took the rap for another crime committed by the killer or killers of the triangle women, obscuring the true pattern. In Northern Ireland alone, eighty-four convictions were quashed in the ten years between 2007 and 2017, so wrongful charges do occur. There must have been many more during the panic and fog of the Troubles, as we've seen in the Guildford Four and Birmingham Six cases.

We also don't know if 1998 really marked the end of the crimes – it's possible that's wrong too. A girl was murdered in December that year, her body left on a beach in Galway. It's the other side of the country, and the wrong MO, and a man's in prison for that murder, but he's always said he's innocent and is demanding the DNA be re-tested. Inside the triangle, a teenager named Raonaid (the Irish for Rachel) Murray, only seventeen, was killed just outside Dublin in September 1999, walking home late at night to change her clothes before going out to a disco. She was stabbed multiple times in a frenzied attack. As in many of these cases, there's a chief suspect, who lived nearby and was possibly seen arguing with her that night, but they have never been charged and the murder is still officially unsolved. While it's a different MO from the triangle cases, it's in the same area and just a year after the last of those cases, so surely it should have been looked at. Raonaid's sister found her body, which was just fifty yards from her home, about an hour after she was killed. There are rumours of a cover-up in this case too, of a high-profile killer protected by the Gardaí. Or incompetence, crucial mistakes made in the early stages – claims upheld by a cold-case review in 2008. Last year, on the twentieth anniversary of her death, her family once again asked someone to come forward if they knew something, anything at all. No one did.

So there are at least two cases from this same period where the Gardaí made serious mistakes. Other mistakes could easily have been made in the triangle cases, that allowed a killer to go free.

In the books I write, detectives are always tenacious, laser-focused, working the case at the cost of their personal life. In real life this doesn't always happen, and maybe it shouldn't. All the same, you'd like to think that if you were murdered or abducted, no stone would be left unturned. Operation Trace certainly overturned a lot of stones, and interviewed a lot of people, followed a lot of leads. Ultimately, however, no one was arrested. No real progress was made. After three years, the task force shut up shop, although for the detectives it was never really over. Every time another woman was killed or raped or went missing, they would be watching. Paying attention. Knowing there was a good chance the man they sought was already on their radar, that maybe they'd already interviewed him and they just couldn't prove anything. Knowing that if someone was out there, he'd likely do it again.

As we drank our teas on that rainy day in Dublin, I asked Alan if he felt he'd done his best. He said yes, because they had done everything they could. But also no, because 'We didn't find the girls.' I can only imagine how this would haunt you: if I'd just talked to that one other person; if I'd just pressed that little bit harder; if I'd chased down that random lead, that rumour, that crackpot tip. But there were so many rumours and so many tips. So many of the women are being searched for even now, twenty years on, fields dug up and houses excavated. Alan says he believes that the cases will be solved one day, but probably not through finding the bodies by chance, although it's always possible. He puts the ongoing impasse down to the fact that some people are too scared to talk. Maybe there's a woman out there who's been in a relationship with a violent man, a man she's afraid of. Maybe, as in the case of Vincent Connell's girlfriend back in the eighties, the police asked her and her partner questions while they were in the room together. He said he was with her at a crucial time when a murder took place, and she agreed, too frightened to do otherwise. Maybe it haunts some other woman, the fact that a small lie she told could have let her man go free. Maybe he sleeps beside her at night, and she wonders – could it be? Is it possible?

The men we've seen so far as suspects and convicted killers and rapists, Larry Murphy, John Crerar, David Lawler, even Robert Howard, had wives, and young children too in most cases. They were hiding in plain sight, except that when you scratch the surface, there's always a woman with a story to tell. A clumsy lunge in a car from a man she trusted, and she buried the shock, not wanting to upset people, perhaps blaming herself to some extent. It's what women are taught to do by the multiple rape trials that bring as evidence the way we acted that night, the underwear we wore. There's a spectrum of stories all the way from a dodgy feeling to a fully fledged rape, when either a woman told her story and wasn't believed, or, worse, she was believed and he still didn't serve any time, or he was released in a handful of years, ready to do it again. However, Alan still holds out hope, even though it's more than twenty years since Operation Trace was set up, with the resources and will to achieve results, but still not getting them. Perhaps one day that fear will end, the hold that whoever has over a witness will pass, the relationship will end or the man will die, and they will feel able to speak out about what they know. Maybe then the women can be found and brought home. Maybe.

Chapter Nine

So, Who Did It?

It's a good story, the vanishing triangle – eight women missing in the same area – and it took years for anyone to even connect them. A serial killer operating in Ireland, and getting away with it because no one realised. Beautiful, vulnerable young women, snatched off the streets or from their homes. Ireland is a small place even now. How could so many bodies be concealed for so long? Ireland is a gossipy place, a nosy place. How could no one have noticed a husband or father or friend acting strangely? How could nobody see Deirdre Jacob taken almost from her front door, or Imelda Keenan from a street in broad daylight? They noticed when Jastine Valdez was taken in 2018, and tried to save her, but it was too late. Has Ireland just changed in all this time? Are people more willing to call the police, to speak out – or has something as simple as mobile phones made all the difference? Would the farmer who burned Fiona Sinnott's things do something different nowadays – see it on the constant rolling stream of news and social media we all live immersed in, call it in right away instead of burning the evidence? Would the names of the people suspected of killing Fiona Pender, Fiona Sinnott and Ciara Breen have been leaked on Twitter at the time? Would the phones each of the women would inevitably have owned have yielded clues about where they went, their last movements, who they were meeting? As we all know from watching crime shows on TV, you have to switch a phone right off, take the battery out, for it to be untraceable. Surely they would be found, if it happened now. If not alive, then at least their bodies.

When I first heard about these cases, I learned the six names of the women in Operation Trace, names I had never heard before despite being a teenage girl in Ireland while all this was happening. Then I realised there were at least two more who weren't included. Three, if you count Arlene Arkinson, and I can't see why some miles of geography should mean we don't. Then I learned that there were still others, women whose bodies did turn up, by whatever quirk of bad or good luck. Is it lucky to have your body found? Jo Jo Dullard's sister certainly feels the family would be lucky to find her, so painful is it to know she's out there somewhere, unfound.

As I researched, the ways in which the women disappeared or were killed began to cluster. Out for a walk alone, or running errands in the daytime – Annie, Imelda, Deirdre, Eva. Taking a lift from the wrong person, perhaps – Arlene, Jo Jo, Antoinette Smith. Pulled into a car – Jastine, the unnamed woman in Carlow, maybe some of the others. From their own homes – both Fionas, Ciara. Close to Christmas – Patricia, Marilyn, Sophie, Imelda again. The novelist in me wants this Christmas connection to be a real link, not just a coincidence given higher levels of violence at that booze-soaked time of year. But again, we just don't know. So what are we supposed to do to keep ourselves safe? Not leave the house in daylight? Not get a lift, in a country with scarce public transport? Not stay at home? Not love a man?

I've looked over all these cases in detail, and even extended the vanishing triangle wider, because, as I keep saying, Ireland is a small place. Its borders are largely imaginary, and they have been for decades.

This story is different from those featured in podcasts such as *Serial* or *West Cork* (both murders that also took place in the nineties, incidentally, in 1999 and 1996, although one was in America). There were suspects in each of those cases, which we don't have for most of the ones here, although we can speculate, and there were bodies. With bodies, you know it's murder. You have DNA, clues. You have a timeline. In the cases of the vanished women, we don't have any of those things. We don't even know for sure they are dead, though it seems sadly inevitable. So all I can do is conjecture, like everyone else has done.

Personally, I think that yes, there was a serial killer, which by definition involves three or more murders at different times. I think this person killed as many as five of the triangle women, and perhaps carried out some of the earlier murders as well. If I had to guess, I'd say that both Fionas were killed by people they knew, and trusted. They weren't snatched by a random stranger off the street. With Ciara Breen too, it seems likely she was killed by the man she went to meet that night, the one who, years later, took an overdose in police custody and died. As for the other cases looked at by Operation Trace – Deirdre, Jo Jo, Annie – I believe they were taken by a stranger, maybe snatched off the road. Perhaps in Annie's case by someone she struck up a conversation with on her day out – maybe that man at the pub. In Jo Jo's case, she probably got into a car with the wrong person. I believe something happened to Eva Brennan too, that she met someone on the road that day, maybe was also offered a lift. As her family said, if she did kill herself, where is her body? She couldn't bury herself. Imelda Keenan – if the story told about her last sighting is true, it's likely she was also snatched off the street. That makes at least five women, not to mention the ones we know are dead, found buried in the same area, whose murders have never been solved. So if there was one killer, who was it?

I knew pretty early on that I would not be able to 'solve' these cases. If the Gardaí couldn't after more than twenty years, I certainly can't. In the crime novels I write, there is always a solution, of course. The questions would be answered, the mysteries unravelled, and we'd know where these women are and what happened to them, who hurt them. Real life doesn't work that way. If I were writing this as a novel, we'd be able to prove the women were abducted and killed by the same person – perhaps Larry Murphy, who took a woman with such practised ease in 2000. As soon as he was convicted of the violent rape mentioned in the prologue, he became an obvious suspect in the triangle cases. He'd snatched a woman off the street, driven her into the Wicklow Mountains, raped her and been in the process of murdering her when he was interrupted. It seemed unlikely, given the speed and savagery of the attack, that he had never done it before. He was a hunter, and he knew the mountains well enough to navigate in the dark, find the secret places. He strikes me as an American kind of villain, with his guns and his strength, not someone you'd find in Ireland. Yet somehow this was the first time the carpenter, a married man with kids, had ever come to the attention of Gardaí. When arrested, he said, 'I don't know why I did it,' but when confronted with the pain he'd caused his victim, he pointed out she was at least still alive. Meaning his other victims weren't? Operation Trace was not able to connect him to any of the disappearances, and so we come back to the same problem: without bodies, there is only so much that can be done.

There was a possible link, very faint, between Larry Murphy and Annie McCarrick. When he was finally caught, in 2000, a rumour went round that Murphy, a carpenter, had been working on the roof of Johnnie Fox's pub that week in 1993. No proof was ever found of this, but certainly Murphy did travel the country working as a carpenter and on building sites, of which there were many in the nineties. The Gardaí also found that he liked to steal souvenirs such as bank statements from the homes of women he worked for, a noted habit of serial killers. However, he wouldn't say if he'd ever met Annie, and there was no way to take the theory further, so it remains just speculation. Larry Murphy was linked to Eva Brennan's case too, if only through speculation: her sister Colette recalled that her father's pub, which Eva lived opposite, was being renovated at the time of her disappearance, and Murphy was known to do work like that. Once again though, the evidence was too slight to take further. Barely even evidence, really. One marginally stronger link was that, when Deirdre Jacob's grandmother died, a flyer was found among her possessions with Larry Murphy's details on it. Deirdre had gone to see her grandmother on the day she went missing – was she on Murphy's radar? Again, a very slight link, and he wouldn't tell the Gardaí anything. However, he remains the top suspect in several of the cases, and it's also notable that there were no more disappearances in the triangle after he was arrested in 2000.

Larry Murphy was released from prison in 2010, and there was outcry when it was rumoured he'd return to live in Baltinglass, not far from where the women were still missing. His brother took the step of declaring that Larry would not be welcome back with his family. Murphy apparently lives in London now, after spells in Spain and Amsterdam. He appeared to get on well in prison, making furniture for the officers, and seeming in good spirits, despite the fact his family didn't visit him once during his sentence. He refused to take part in any rehabilitation programmes, and told Gardaí nothing when they questioned him about the earlier disappearances.

Then there's John Crerar, who killed a woman savagely in 1979 and was free for twenty years to do it again. He left Phyllis Murphy's body to be found and eventually convict him. Maybe he decided not to make that mistake again. Like so many of these men, he'd been accused by three different women of assaulting them when they were children, but nothing ever came of it. He worked as a security guard on the Aga Khan's stud farm, behind which was a quarry where waste was often dumped. People said they saw things there, heard things, like screams late at night. Smelled decay, even. But nothing was ever found. There was no proof, other than the words of young girls, which as we've seen never held much weight in Ireland. There's even been some suggestion that two people were involved in these crimes – one to pull a woman into a car, one to drive – and that Murphy and Crerar knew each other, that they had been seen together near the quarry behind Crerar's work the night after Jo Jo Dullard went missing. But that's just speculation and, as we know, people misremember things, they get dates wrong, they embellish. It is rare but not unknown for killers to work together. By the start of the next decade, when the disappearances apparently stopped, both Crerar and Murphy had been arrested.

One chilling little detail is that David Lawler, who murdered Marilyn Rynn in 1995, as she walked home from a night out, also knew Larry Murphy. Some reports say they were cousins, and certainly they had been at school together, in the same year, and in prison, after Larry was convicted of rape, they became friends. Is this just another example of Ireland being small, or is there more to it? In another coincidence, David Lawler was found to drink in the same pub as Jo Jo Dullard in Dublin – but he had an alibi for the night she disappeared, having been in the city. It was reported in 2014 that he would be released from prison – he has served over twenty years now – but there was huge public anger that he could be freed after such a brutal murder, and so far he's still inside.

Those are three men known to have raped and murdered, or attempted to murder, women in the triangle area. As we've seen, there were in fact lots of men around Dublin in the nineties who had form for raping and even killing women, or who would go on to do so later. There were men who posed as taxi drivers, and took their passengers out to the Wicklow Mountains to attack them. This may be one way the women were abducted, either getting into what they thought was a cab, trying to be safe as we're always told to be, or else they were duped over to a vehicle and pulled inside. A man called Robert Quigley posed as a taxi driver and took a woman into the Wicklow Mountains after she fell asleep in the back of his car. She woke up to find him strangling her, but when another car passed, he was spooked and stopped his attack. She managed to escape even as he was beating her with a baseball bat – this was in 2006. Although he was only twenty-six at the time of this attack, might he have committed other crimes as a younger man? How old would you have to be to do something like that? Another fake taxi driver, Daniel Moynihan, was just nineteen when he went to prison for raping a woman he'd picked up in 2000, also pretending to be a cab driver, and driven into the same mountains. He was sentenced to twelve years but this was reduced on appeal, and he was soon back on the streets, until he was arrested again for car-jacking several women at knifepoint.

There was also Thomas Callan, from Carrickmacross (not far from Dundalk, where Ciara Breen was taken), who abducted a young woman in 1999. Like Larry Murphy, he put her into the boot of his car and assaulted her, tried to rape her and threatened her with a knife. He had tried to do the same to another girl just a few months before, but she'd managed to get away. He had pretended to be lost, so the girl – who was seventeen – had come over to the car, when he bundled her in and drove her out to the country. He was only twenty-one at the time. Again, is that too young to have done anything to the other women?

Coincidentally, another cousin of Larry Murphy's, a man called Thomas Dalton, was jailed for sexual assault in 2010. He got only a year in prison for this – and not until five years after the attack, which took place in 2005 – and the victim said she'd felt as if she were on trial herself. Why does it take so long for cases to come to court? Why do we let these violent men go free; serve so little time?

Robert Howard is another key suspect in the triangle cases. He was the last person to see Arlene Arkinson alive, and he died in prison in 2015 after murdering a teenage girl in London. Before that, Howard had moved around a lot. He'd even been living near to where Fiona Sinnott went missing, close to the ferry port, although this was probably after Fiona's disappearance. As we've heard, he was never convicted of killing Arlene, and so never revealed where her body was. Howard had a long history of hurting women. He had apparently held another girl, who had some learning difficulties, hostage in a caravan for several days, abusing her too. His original MO was to break into houses and take a woman by surprise, then later he progressed to grooming a girl, then holding her captive while he assaulted her. So here you have a man who is known to hurt women, both young and old, and he gives a young girl a lift and she's never seen again, yet you still can't convict him. You can't convict him even while he's in prison for killing another girl of the same age. I wonder if Howard – the Wolfman, as he called himself – used the border as a way to draw a line under what he'd done, and start again in Ireland, or in England, knowing that the forces didn't talk to each other. He lived all over Ireland, where he was even married for a few years, as well as in Glasgow, where he reportedly moved to get away from the flack surrounding Arlene's disappearance. He was given a council flat there, claiming he was on the run from the IRA. He then moved to London, where he was introduced to Hannah Williams by a woman he dated for a while, before murdering Hannah and going to prison. I wonder how many unsolved missing persons cases there are in those cities, how many girls went out one day and never came home.

And there's Mark Hennessy, who in 2018 dragged Jastine Valdez off the street and into his car on a spring evening, and within less than an hour had strangled her. It was the Wicklow Mountains again. It echoed the way police thought some of the women had been taken. Jo Jo Dullard, for example, looking for a lift, or Deirdre Jacob walking along the road in broad daylight. Had he done it before? He was dead, so they couldn't ask him, but people wondered. However, he would have been fifteen years old when Annie McCarrick went missing in 1993. Too young, surely, to have had anything to do with it. Since he's gone, we'll never know for sure.

As discussed, one theory is that two men worked together to take women. It wouldn't have been the first time – a pair of men in the 1970s had roamed the country, killing two women. Perhaps that explains why police could never pin the crimes on one particular person. Thomas Stokes and Adrian Power were two possible suspects on the Gardaí's radar in the nineties, known to have been in the area for several of the disappearances, such as Jo Jo and Ciara. They were cousins from the travelling community, who had taken a sex worker up to the mountains and raped her over several hours on the night of 29 December 1994 (Christmas again). The rape had taken place near Enniskerry – the same place Annie McCarrick was last seen in 1993. The attack was brutal, and the woman, who had two children, was sure she wouldn't make it out of the car alive, especially as they called each other by their names in front of her. One of them bit her on the shoulder, right through the skin (I note that biting has occurred in a number of these cases I've mentioned). They were convicted of this crime and jailed, but not until 1996 for Stokes and 1999 for Powers. I can't see why this could possibly have taken so long. In 1999 Stokes offered to help Gardaí with the Deirdre Jacob investigation, though he'd been in jail for years at that point so it's not clear what he said he knew, and, like everything in these cases, it came to nothing anyway.

Back in 1987, Gardaí believed that Antoinette Smith had been killed by the two men in the taxi with her, who would probably have had to carry her body up to the bog where they buried her. She was found only because the weather had been dry, and the landscape shifted; you have to wonder if the same will happen for any of the other women, if Antoinette's name would have been added to this list of the missing except for blind luck. If you can call it luck, to have your body found in a bog. The same was true of Marie Kilmartin, found dead in 1993 – the police thought two people would have been needed to bury her like that, deep in a bog with heavy items left on top of her grave. Witnesses had also apparently seen Jo Jo Dullard at different locations, in a wood and in a car with two men, trying to run away and being pulled back by her hair. In 2002 a psychic gave an interview to Irish press where she said she was sure two people, men in their thirties, were involved in the disappearances. It's an interesting fact that psychics have been used in several of these cases – Irish people perhaps being more open to such things. In 1998, just a month after Deirdre Jacob went missing, a young woman was almost abducted by a man in a car ten miles from Carlow, where Larry Murphy would strike two years later. She described the man as well built, very strong, around thirty – and she said he'd been stalking her along with another man earlier that day. She was lucky to get away, as he ripped a hole in her T-shirt trying to pull her into the car.

Larry Murphy's brother, Thomas, gave an interview where he said Larry's actions had destroyed the family, and although he wasn't sure if his brother had been involved in the disappearances, he had asked him about them, and also couldn't be sure that he hadn't. Larry's out of prison now, as I said, and has been living free since 2010. John Crerar's still in jail, as is David Lawler. Robert Howard died there, Mark Hennessy was shot by the police. And perhaps there is another man, one who's never come to police attention, hiding as Larry Murphy did all those years, apparently a model citizen. A man whose name might cross the mind of a woman when she hears about another girl killed or missing, and she might wonder, what if? After all, there was the thing he did to her. Maybe she never told anyone, or maybe she did and wasn't believed. Maybe women have whispered his name to each other, in the dark – *be careful of that one*. Maybe he'll come to light one day, but probably not until another woman is hurt or killed.

It's striking the names used for these men: the Beast of Baltinglass, Larry Murphy; Robert 'Wolfman' Howard; the Beast of Bray, Mark Hennessy; Michael 'the Monster' Murphy, the man who killed Bettina Poeschel and who had killed before, and who was free during at least some of the nineties, released from prison in 1992 after murdering a woman only eight years before. Nicknames that portray them as animals, predators rising out of the darkness. As if they can't help themselves. As it is, there are plenty of men who have killed, raped and hurt women in Ireland, many during the period when these women went missing. Although we'll never know until someone talks, it's clear that lenient sentencing has played a role in many of them being free to do it again.

There are a lot of names in this chapter – meaning there are a lot of violent men in Ireland. When I realised this, I began to feel quite naïve for assuming I'd grown up in a safe country. In a novel, I would have to settle on one suspect and I'd probably go for Larry Murphy, top of most people's lists, known to pull women into cars, known to be violent and murderous. In fiction, he would be convicted of all these crimes and go to jail for life, instead of being released after nine years, and not even put on the Sex Offenders Register. In reality, I don't know who did it – it could have been any of these men. I find it hard to believe John Crerar, for example, didn't rape or murder again during those twenty years. I think we can discount Mark Hennessy as being too young, and others for not being around during the relevant years. So maybe Crerar, or Murphy, or both together. Or else each woman was killed by a different person, who has somehow managed to cover it up all this time. I can't decide which would be worse.

Chapter Ten

Now: Two Murders

As I keep saying, the nineties in Ireland was a time of huge change. We were told by Tony Blair that the hand of history was on his shoulder back in 1998, but in truth things were changing in all kinds of ways, not just politically. Socially. Technologically. Religiously. By the end of the millennium, the damage to the Catholic Church from all the scandals was so extreme that it was being talked of as dead and gone in Ireland. This in a country seen as the last bastion of the faith, at least until the eighties. There were scandals not just about child abuse, but also about the horrific conditions in children's homes run by nuns and priests, as well as mother and baby homes; also the practice of baby selling, where Irish women had their babies taken and adopted by wealthy American Catholics. Vocations to the priesthood had dropped by 92 per cent since the sixties, and as people began to recognise the hypocrisy of the Church, attitudes softened towards those who had slipped. Even the Prime Minister from 1997 onwards, Bertie Ahern, was divorced, living with a partner he wasn't married to. No one cared about this too much, it seemed. It was a new country.

Towards the end of the decade, the economy had also gone mad. In 1998 Ireland joined the euro, its economy soaring, as if it would never crash back down. There was virtually full employment and growth was at 9 per cent for five years – the Celtic Tiger economy, as it was called. Some areas around Dublin – the vanishing triangle areas – saw their population triple in five years. In a total reversal of the trend since the famine, when the population declined by 3 million within just a few years, people were moving to Ireland from other countries. This meant more people, more crime and also more places to hide bodies, as Ireland experienced an unprecedented construction boom. Perhaps it isn't surprising, then, that the nineties also saw so many cases of women going missing, or being found dead. It's a demographic issue, in part. But there are a lot of women all the same.

Fast-forward twenty years, to summer 2018. Things had supposedly changed even more in Ireland. The abortion referendum, for all it stirred up gross misogyny, had passed with a comfortable margin. There was a gay Prime Minister, and between 1990 and 2011, the President had always been a woman. But in May 2018, Jastine Valdez was abducted off the road in Enniskerry – the same village Annie McCarrick was most likely heading to in 1993 when the last verified sighting of her was made. Jastine was taken after getting off the bus, on a busy road where it would still have been light at that time of year, and she was dead probably within the hour. Earlier that day she had gone to renew her residency permit, then to the gym, then bought a loaf of bread as her mother had requested. She had last messaged her mother two hours before, the sixty-third message they'd exchanged that day via Facebook. This says so much about how close they must have been, despite spending most of Jastine's life apart. The bread and her phone, smashed, were found at the side of the road. There was a manhunt, and the next day, a Sunday, someone spotted the same car she'd been pushed into, parked in a business park outside town. Around eight o'clock in the evening, police approached. They saw the driver had a knife, and was waving it about, and thought Jastine was in the car with him and about to be killed, so they fired a shot which went through his shoulder. He died. He'd left a note, now bloodstained, with a place name written on it, along with the word 'sorry'. The next day, police found Jastine's body there. She had been raped and strangled, and had a small amount of cocaine in her blood, although her boyfriend said she would never have touched drugs unless they'd been forced on her. Two people dead, killer and victim, within one weekend.

This case had a different outcome in so many ways from the other ones in this book – there were witnesses, for a start. It was clear right away she'd been abducted rather than simply slipping out of her life. There were cameras on the bus, which had even picked up the make of the killer's car – it appeared he might have been following it. Her killer, Mark Hennessy, must have known he couldn't get away with it, which is perhaps why he made his last stand against police. This kind of thing rarely happens in Ireland, where most police officers are not routinely armed (even in the much larger UK, only three people were shot by police last year). At the recent inquest, his wife said he'd gone out that evening to buy a bottle of wine, then didn't come home all night. Early next morning, she rang him, and he told her he'd slept in his car. He seemed fine, she said. He would be dead by the end of the day. I wonder how it was for her, too, to realise she'd married a man like that, when Gardaí came to her door not long after that phone call, having traced his address already. It shows how easy detection can be in the modern world. Witnesses described a car, and within hours police had a list of everyone in the area who owned that make. Soon he'd be dead, and she'd never know why he did it. His wife has now left the country with her kids, I imagine hoping to start again, if you ever could after something like that.

Mark Hennessy was forty, with two children – same as Larry Murphy. Also like Murphy, he had never been arrested or convicted of anything before. Because this crime took place in 2018 and not earlier, there's even video footage of him right before the attack, clear and sharp. He walks across the pub car park to his black car, in jeans and a blue T-shirt. He looks purposeful, in shape, young for his age although his hair is close-cropped. He hadn't been drinking, people said, although it would later turn out he often used cocaine, that he had Tinder on his phone despite being married. But in this video, as he reverses his car out of the pub car park, there's nothing to suggest anger, or lust, or the kind of madness that would see him pull a woman into his car just half an hour later. He even went back to the pub that evening, around eleven, after he'd killed and dumped Jastine, and chatted to people again, appearing normal.

The first question to ask was why. The attack was seemingly random, vicious; just before, he had been in the pub with friends, and no one noticed any agitation. Mark seemed slightly bored, if anything. He ate some crisps and left after about ten minutes, saying the football match on TV, the FA Cup Final, was dull. Around forty-five minutes later, he spotted Jastine on the road. He saw her and he took her, and raped her, and murdered her in less than an hour. We'll never know why. Had he carried this savagery in him all his life, only for it to erupt on this May evening? Had he done this before? RTE news had a video of him hanging out with friends in a pub, recorded a week before he murdered Jastine. He appears smiling, cheerful, a fun man. Good craic, as we'd say in Ireland. Nothing to suggest he could do this kind of thing. It was a mystery, a savage one.

As shocking as her death was, Jastine was not the first woman to be violently murdered in Ireland that year, she was actually the fourth (and all this by May). In another case that rocked Ireland, Ana, or Anastasia, Kriegel was raped and murdered by two of her classmates in Dublin a week before Jastine was taken. Ana was fourteen and the boys who killed her were thirteen. She had more than fifty injuries to her body when Gardaí found her, after three days, in an abandoned, almost pitch-dark, filthy building. She had fought hard for her life. Ana had been adopted from Russia and was fighting even before the attack, to have friends, to be happy. It was all taken away from her after the boys lured her there. It seemed the boy who took the lead had amped himself up on violent porn and computer games, and had planned what he was going to do. The savagery of the attack, from such young boys, left the country reeling. While researching Marilyn Rynn's murder, it struck me it must have been one of the first where internet porn played a role. In 1995, hardly anyone in Ireland had the internet – we got it at home in 1999, but it was very slow and expensive – so to have been using it to view porn at this stage, as her killer, David Lawler, was, is unusual. When they examined Lawler's computer, Gardaí noticed an escalation in the material he'd been watching. The violence, the darkness of it, feeding off itself. One of the teenage boys in the Ana Kriegel murder case had also downloaded thousands of violent and pornographic images, all available on his own mobile phone. It's hard to say that watching such things makes you more likely to lure a girl or a woman to a quiet place, then rape and beat and murder her, as happened in both these cases. But we can say that the boy looked at images he later acted out on Ana. That violence against women was on his mind, within his world view.

Jastine Valdez was taken off the street, and it's not known if she had ever met Mark Hennessy, if he had seen her somewhere and been stalking her or not. Most likely it was a random abduction by a stranger, just like we're always warned about. But the other three women killed that year were murdered by people they knew:

one by her husband, one by her ex-husband, and Ana Kriegel, a girl of just fourteen, by boys from her school. These women, and this girl, should instead have feared their partners, the boys they went to school with, heads full of the violent porn they watched on their phones. Women's Aid Ireland have started cataloguing what they call femicides in the country. TV and film, crime podcasts, our parents, they all teach us to be afraid of serial killers, of strangers in the dark offering lifts, of walking home alone at night. And yet according to the Women's Aid report of 2019, of the over 200 women murdered violently in Ireland since records started in 1996, 87 per cent of them knew their killer. In 2019, five women were violently murdered in Ireland, three by their partners, and one by her son. The fifth was also reportedly killed by a man she knew.

◆　◆　◆

When I started writing this book, I was surprised to note that quite a few relevant events had taken place in 2018 and 2019. As well as another triangle murder, that of Jastine, in the last year or two there has also been progress on older, unsolved cases. Inga Hauser, a German tourist killed back in the eighties, was eighteen when she was murdered. She was killed in Northern Ireland, taken probably minutes after getting off the ferry from Scotland, and her body lay abandoned in woodland for weeks. Although this was over thirty years ago, last year – 2019 – a man was questioned by police. It shows these old cases are still live, doggedly pursued by detectives often long retired. There is DNA in Inga's case, should they ever find the right suspect. And who's to say that whoever took her off the country road didn't do this to other women over the years? Maybe her killer can still be caught. After I wrote this section – in November 2019 – I looked up the case on the BBC website, to see if there had been any more progress, only to find that Inga's mother, Almut, had sadly died the month before. Another parent gone without ever finding answers, or peace. The same story reported that a file on the case had been sent to the PPS (our version of the CPS because, again, words have weight here, and 'Crown' is a heavy one) in June 2019. Maybe there will be progress next year. Always maybe.

◆ ◆ ◆

Likewise, in many of the other cases, searches were made, appeals issued, witnesses questioned. There was an inquest into Arlene Arkinson's death, and a renewed search for her. There were also new investigations in the cases of Fiona Sinnott and Ciara Breen, fresh searches that sadly led nowhere, looking in the foundations of houses and in fields and bogs. In 2019 a body was found near where Fiona Sinnott had gone missing, a woman's. This proved to be an Italian woman who'd been travelling round Ireland, and she'd been there for a year or so undiscovered, but there had been no foul play, Gardaí said. There were numerous developments in the murder of Sophie Toscan du Plantier, as her family sought to have Ian Bailey extradited. But time is running out for some. Inga Hauser's mother died in 2019 as we've seen – her father had died in 2006, again before his time, again broken-hearted. Likewise, Eva Brennan's sister Colette died in 2016. Fiona Pender's mother died in 2017, Ciara Breen's in 2018, as well as Jo Jo's sister Mary and Fiona Sinnott's sister Caroline.

Ireland has changed so much since the nineties. But, nonetheless, it has not changed enough. It's still a country that reflects deep hatred and contempt towards women, even as it worships them in the form of the Virgin Mary, the spotless mother. As we've seen, there were two high-profile rape cases in 2018, both ending in acquittal and sparking off widespread protests at the treatment of the women involved. Just this week I'm reading an article from Limerick, where a young man was convicted of breaking into a woman's home and raping her in bed, but received no jail time. The judge said he hoped the woman could just 'put it behind her'. This is the country we still live in, both north and south of the border. In Northern Ireland, a handful of zealots have done their best to make sure we retain fundamentalist abortion laws and no equal marriage, propped up ably by a bunch of shameless Tory MPs. Finally, as of 2020, this situation is over. You can't hold back progress, not when the people want it enough.

◆　◆　◆

On 4 December 2019 I flew over to Dublin to attend the seventh Annual Missing Persons Day. I was nervous as I walked there in the pearly Dublin light – I was going to come face to face with people who'd suffered so much. The women I'd been writing about, and reading about for years – they had known these women. Been in rooms with them, living and breathing, seen them every day for years, and now they were just . . . gone. Perhaps that's why missing persons cases often capture the public imagination so much – there's a dark sorcery to it, like the magician in a vanishing case, or sawing a woman in half. Where did they go? How can so many people just disappear, in a small country where everyone knows each other? The event was held in a large, wood-panelled room, hung with portraits of various important men I didn't recognise. A choir of schoolchildren sang. During the remembrance ceremony, they talked first about some good news. A new project to DNA-test relatives of missing people, and match them with unidentified bodies, found not just in Ireland but all over the UK, has yielded results. A number of missing people were discovered buried in nameless graves in Wales, where the locals had looked after them for years after their bodies washed up there. I found this quite moving. So there is progress, however small. There is hope, but there is so much pain and loss as well.

In the break, I spoke to two people whose relatives had gone missing overseas. Gary's cousin Peter Wilson vanished in 2019 while in Tenerife. Helen's brother James (JP) Grealis has been missing in the Netherlands since 2008. She spoke of their frustrations with the Dutch police, who had taken years to interview key witnesses, and the difficulties with the language barrier, with having to rely on a foreign police service. Both described that same state peculiar to families of the missing, where you're grieving, except grief relies on certainty and you don't even have that. You're just stuck, waiting to feel the wound that's been inflicted on you.

I also spoke to Ciaran Baxter, who along with his brother Martin, found their missing brother Ronan alive in London in 2005. Ciaran has written a book about their search, called *Bring Him Home*. Ronan had been suffering from mental health problems, and had gone missing from the family in Cork. As he didn't have a passport, they assumed he couldn't have left the country, so thought he must be in Dublin, which at least he knew well. He had come off his medication, and had little money, so the family were frantic. By chance, they were able to view CCTV from Cork airport on the day Ronan had gone missing, though they thought he couldn't have travelled anywhere by plane without ID. They also knew there was only one flight a day to London, and there was no sign of him in the airport around then. Next the family set in motion a massive media campaign – and it paid off when someone reported seeing Ronan at the airport that day, but later on, in the evening. What the family didn't know – and no one had told them – was that the one flight to London had been delayed that day, by several hours. They viewed the CCTV from the later time period and there he was, clearly visible. Despite only having a bus pass and hardly any money, Ronan had somehow gone to London, and so his brothers went after him.

They spent weeks hunting, approaching groups of homeless people, putting up posters, contacting the media, and even enlisting the help of the Irish Embassy. Eventually they found their brother, only a few Tube stops along from Heathrow, where he'd arrived in the country. Again, this happened because a woman saw his picture in the paper and then recognised him in a nearby park, and called the police. He had been sleeping rough, not taking his meds, and the brothers felt they had found him just in time, or he wouldn't have survived. Luckily, it was the summer, and warm out. He had been missing for only five weeks, but who knows what the outcome might have been otherwise.

This took place nearly fifteen years ago, but it clearly weighs heavily on the family, how close they came to losing him for ever, to him being another name among the lost. If they hadn't known he went to London, they would have been looking in the wrong place, in Dublin most likely. I also wonder if he'd have been found had they not physically gone to London to look for him, with the help of the Met police, media and Irish Embassy. Ciaran confirmed that he thought this happy outcome was a result of all the help they'd received – finding out by a tip-off and CCTV that Ronan had left the country, for example, when this should not have been possible – and the fact they had actually gone to London and tracked him down.

This story has a lot to say about tenacity, and about not making assumptions in missing persons cases – that someone without a passport could not get out of Ireland, that a plane had left when it was supposed to, that someone would have told the family if this was not the case. Granted, Ronan had gone missing of his own accord (in as much as he was capable of that at the time), and no one had tried to hurt him, no one had dragged him off the street into a car. There was also more CCTV around in 2005 than in the nineties, which was a big help, and more people had mobile phones, although Ronan didn't. But it does go to show that people sometimes can be found, if no stone is left unturned.

During the day I also spoke to a woman whose brother had gone missing over fifty years ago – he was then not quite nine years old. It was the first time she'd come to the missing persons event. Fifty years of missing someone: imagine that.

In the speeches, a sister of another missing person, Lisa Dorrian, spoke eloquently about Lisa, and what they think happened to her – that she was murdered. Lisa was from County Down, Northern Ireland, and went missing in 2005. She was twenty-five, a beautiful blonde. She'd gone to a party at a caravan park, and the people she was with – one a teenage boy – said they had heard noises, and gone outside and 'lost her in the dark'. No trace of her has been found since. There were rumours she had been killed by Loyalist Paramilitary group the LVF, although the Troubles were supposedly long over at this point. It's another of those cases where people locally could tell you names, and probably have a good idea what transpired but won't say. The LVF was the group responsible for many of the killings in the latter days of the Troubles, right up to the end. The police – by then the PSNI, since, as mentioned, the RUC was disbanded in 2001 – brought in helicopters, searched the water, as they thought Lisa might have been put in the sea. In 2015 a serving prisoner gave some information about where she might be buried, but it came to nothing. As recently as 2019, the PSNI were again searching near the caravan site where Lisa was last seen. She is officially considered one of the Disappeared, although she went missing decades after the others on that list. Her family were desperate, her sister Joanne said, and had even turned to psychics to try to locate Lisa's body. Their mother died four years ago, not even sixty, and they believe her heart was broken. Many of the families say the same thing – that the missing person is not the only family member who's lost when they disappear.

Joanne kindly spoke to me at the end of the day, and she agreed that the border seemed to have hampered the creation of a cohesive missing persons policy for Ireland, and that they felt quite isolated, being in the North. That even less was done for them than for those in the South. Joanne, who's maybe my age or younger, is blonde and pretty like her sister, and spoke with confidence and dignity at the event. Her family are sure that people know what happened to Lisa, but, once again, no one is talking. Out of fear maybe, or loyalty, or that familiar Irish silence.

Jo Jo Dullard's surviving sister, Kathleen, also got up and spoke, quiet and composed. She said Jo Jo had had her whole life ahead of her, and that it was taken away by someone. Her other sister Mary and brother Tom have died without knowing what became of her, and she described this as 'the cruellest form of torture'. They still hope they will find something out, but the weariness is evident, after so many years. As Ireland's golden-boy poet, Yeats, wrote: 'Too long a sacrifice can make a stone of the heart'.

In the middle of the day, there was a slideshow of some of the almost 900 people missing in Ireland. It was overwhelming. I was struck by how many men have gone missing, especially young men, and often while travelling overseas. Although this book focuses on women, it's clear that men are also facing violence and mental health crises, and that they may not have as many social or family ties as women, making it easier to slip away, to become lost. It's a truly staggering number when you see it like that, a parade of names and faces, each one representing a broken family.

People I spoke to mentioned various measures that might help when you have a missing relative. Automatically getting assigned a family liaison officer, which I was surprised to hear doesn't always happen. Some families have been left in the dark about investigations, to find their way through it alone. More support would help, they said. Counselling. Information. Some praised the PSNI or Gardaí and some were less satisfied. In most cases people seemed to assume they were looking for a body rather than a living person, and they desperately wanted to find their relative and bury them. 'A Christian burial' is a term that comes up a lot – in Ireland, this matters. What's clear is that the problem of missing people is not a nineties issue, left behind like hostility to unmarried mothers or contraception.

Barry Cummins, a well-known journalist who MCed the day and has written extensively about missing persons in Ireland, including the books *Missing* and *Without Trace*, commented that the situation with missing people in Ireland is in fact 'worse than ever'. There was a speech from the Minister for Equality, Immigration and Integration, and also from the Garda Commissioner, Drew Harris. This was a serious event, full of big hitters. Also there were representatives of the National Missing Persons Helpline, a non-profit organisation trying to help families. Their leaflets advise what to do when someone is missing: contact the police; find a recent photo and describe them; check if their passport is gone, if any money has been taken out of accounts, if they've got their phone, clothes, keys and so on; use social media and put up posters, as the Baxter family did so successfully (their brother went missing just before widespread social media).

Although the day was very sad, conversely it reminded me of the warmth and friendliness of Ireland, how easy it is to strike up conversations with people. In all the darkness and sorrow of these stories, that's something to hold on to. I've written a lot of negative things about the country I grew up in, and even that is a complicated statement, because technically I didn't grow up in Ireland, even though I could see it from the windows of our house. I grew up in the United Kingdom, but I've always felt both Irish and

British. In many ways it was a hard and frightening place to be a child, but in other ways I was lucky. There is kindness in this country, and love, and family and community are valued still, which makes it all the more shocking when someone is murdered or goes missing. At the end of the day, homing pigeons were released, birds that know how to get back to where they belong, no matter how far away that is. It was a cold and sunny day, so after watching them fly, fast and sure into the winter sky, everyone went back inside to warm up with soup and tea. Back to their lives, which have to go on somehow.

Epilogue

Since starting to write this book, I have sometimes wondered, a little morbidly, what would happen if I went missing. If the mundane things I might do in an ordinary day – going to the gym or supermarket, messaging a friend – would take on enormous significance. If my last words to a loved one would be something silly, about the weather or if we needed milk. If the clothes I chose to wear that day would be the last I was ever seen in, showing up on grainy CCTV. What picture the media would have of me, if it would be one where I thought I looked ugly. I've become more careful, I think, texting my movements, double-checking the Uber registration. I'm a crime writer so I have a certain dark imagination, but I can't be the only person who's glimpsed myself on a security camera and wondered if that footage might end up in the news if something happened to me. A missing persons case is so endlessly perplexing. Where did they go? If someone didn't take them, was it an accident? Why is there no body if so? Or did they just up and decide to leave their lives, in some cases children, husbands, families? Why would someone do that?

In 2009, a girl came back from the dead. Jaycee Dugard had been living in a compound in a built-up residential neighbourhood for eighteen years. Her family had heard nothing from her since she was taken, aged eleven, in 1991. She had been pulled into a car after being attacked with a kind of stun gun – she'd thought the man was stopping to ask for directions. Her stepfather saw it happen, and pursued the car on a pushbike, but it got away. Her family must have thought she was dead, after so many years. But she came back. She'd lived in hell for almost two decades and yet here she was. She had two teenage children, despite being only twenty-nine herself when she reappeared. She had the first at just fourteen, and didn't even realise she was pregnant, because she'd never been told what sex was. Her daughters were allowed out and about in the world, and had to address her captor's wife, who was complicit in everything, as their mother. After some years, Jaycee was allowed to use the phone, work in the print business her abductor ran, even go out sometimes. When police spoke to Jaycee at the station, after arresting her captor, who had been noticed behaving erratically, she didn't admit who she was for some time. A form of Stockholm Syndrome, perhaps, or a way to survive for so long when you have two children to consider as well. The man had previously served time for abducting and raping a young woman, and police had been at his place several times without spotting Jaycee. All these missed opportunities. They could drive you mad.

There are other names with similar stories. Natasha Kampusch in Austria, taken aged ten, the same year as Deirdre Jacob and Fiona Sinnott went missing, and held for eight years, reappearing in 2006 after being kept in a five-metre-square Cold War bunker under her captor's house. She escaped by chance, when one day she was cleaning her captor's car and he was distracted by a phone call. She ran through the streets, ignored by passers-by, and eventually reached the home of an elderly neighbour, shouting, 'I am Natasha Kampusch.' There's the horrific case of Elisabeth Fritzl, kept in a dungeon by her father for twenty-four years, forced to bear seven of his children, and found when her oldest child, who had lived underground for twenty years, fell ill. Another child will never be able to stand upright, as the cellar ceiling, at five foot six, was lower than his full height. Once again, Josef Fritzl had a conviction for raping another woman, but he had served only one year and his record had been expunged, so no red flags were raised when he and his wife took over the care of several of the children, who Elisabeth had supposedly left at their door. During the time she and the other children were in the basement, over 100 people rented rooms in the Fritzls' home and apparently no one noticed a thing.

Then there's Elizabeth Smart, found in 2003 after having been missing for nine months, abducted at the age of fourteen from her own bedroom, raped every day for that time. She has since married and has three children, is an activist for child safety and has a TV career. Hers is a story full of hope. Then there are the three women imprisoned by Ariel Castro – again held in a residential area for eleven years – found alive when a door was by chance left unlocked and one escaped, who were raped and beaten and terrorised, one forced to bear his child.

I wonder what it's like to hear these stories when you love someone who has been missing for a long time. If it brings you a terrible dart of hope, reignites the awful not knowing, the uncertainty over whether you can mourn them or not. If believing they are dead might actually be easier, without the terrible possibility that maybe they are not.

When I first came across the vanishing triangle cases, I had never heard of them myself, and neither had anyone I mentioned them to – certainly no one in England knew about them. That was in 2013. Since then, podcasts, especially true crime, have doubled in popularity year on year. Everyone has been riveted by the did-he didn't-he case of *Serial*, and then later *West Cork*. There's *My Favorite Murder*, *Last Podcast on the Left*, *Wine and Crime*, and more. So many are run by young women, in a jokey-screamy style, and often themed around drinking. Why is this? Is it to try to gain some measure of control over our fears of what might happen to us – being snatched off the street, or from our own front door? Killed by a man we know, and care for? I wonder sometimes if the joking is distracting from the pain. These women are gone – someone silenced them. They are a dropped phone line, like the one Jo Jo Dullard spoke into before she got into someone's car. They are a letter lost in the post. A gunshot fired but never reaching its target, so their families wait for the pain to hit. We might think that the cruellest thing to do is murder someone, a young innocent woman with her life in front of her. But the families seem to feel it is even crueller to leave them waiting, wondering, hoping. I wonder if the hope is the hardest thing of all.

After all this, I don't know who the killer was, or if there was only one killer, though I can hazard some educated guesses. It's likely it won't be proved unless bodies are found or someone speaks out. Maybe the important point about these cases is not who did it, which we might never know. Maybe it's what they tell us about Ireland, and the world generally, and its attitudes to women. About the kind of people who get looked for when they're missing, or whose murders get priority, and those who don't. About the complacency and judgement directed towards missing women, often by those who should be searching for them. I'm a liberal, but these cases also say a lot about how violent men are able to hurt and even kill women, and then get out of prison, sometimes within just a few years or months, and do it all over again. The reoffending rate for sexual crimes is something like 50 per cent.

Perhaps these are stories about offender management, about sentencing for rape and manslaughter, about the failure of so many reports of sexual violence, about Ireland's rape conviction rate, which has hovered around 1 per cent for years (North and South). About the lengths institutions (the Church, the IRA, sporting clubs, even the police) will go to in order to protect men who matter to them, at the expense of women and children. And, above all, it says something about silence, and secrets. Open secrets, where everyone knows who committed a crime but no one can prove it. Secrets within loving families, like Ciara Breen and her mother. The silence of shame, and guilt, of distrust and fear, which has pervaded Ireland for centuries. Ireland, where the people have a reputation for warmth and chat, is also a silent country, one that far too often seals its lips and eyes to pain. This may be changing. I hope that it is, and that we'll all learn to speak out a little more loudly in future. I also have to hope, as Alan Bailey does, that one day someone will talk, tormented by their conscience, or finally freed from whoever was silencing them.

As we've seen in many of these cases, bodies can be discovered after a long time. Elaine O'Hara was thought to have killed herself until her body was found almost a year later. The availability of CCTV footage also helped a lot. It took months to find Antoinette Smith and Marie Kilmartin. If not for chance, they might have been added to this long list of the women who are still missing. When I attended the annual National Missing Persons Day in December 2019, I was stunned by the sheer number of names and pictures shown on the screen. How can that happen? Where could the bodies be, assuming they are dead? Ireland is small and surrounded by water, and it's not unusual for bodies to surface in rivers, on beaches, in the bog. There was also a lot of building work at that time, as we've seen. So one day some or all of the women may be found. A house could be sold, its foundations dug up, or a tree could be cut down, or, as with Jean McConville, part of the coastline could be eroded and there they are, after so many years. If that happens, the body will tell its own story. There could be DNA, fibres. There might even be possessions that lead us to the killer. DNA might be matched with someone through innocuous means, like the database of a genetic-testing website, as happened for the Golden State Killer, who as far as we know had not attacked or killed anyone since the eighties but was living in the same area, a free man. Who would have thought back then that DNA testing could be used to solve crimes, let alone that it would be so cheap and easy anyone could do it with an at-home kit?

The world changes all the time. Ireland has changed too, so who knows what development, technological or social, may come along and solve these crimes in future. The important thing is not to forget their names, and I hope that this book has allowed a few more people to know them, to remember them. I hope they can be found, and buried, and that some of their relatives will still be alive to know it. It's too late for Bernadette Breen, for Josephine Pender and her husband Sean, and for John McCarrick, Annie's father, for Jo Jo's sister Mary and Imelda Keenan's mother and brother, for Eva Brennan's father and sister, Fiona Sinnott's father and sister, and for all the other relatives who have gone without ever knowing what became of the lost person they loved. I hope it won't be too much longer now.

ACKNOWLEDEGEMENTS

I'd like to thank everyone who spoke to me for this book, especially Pat Marry, Alan Bailey, and Fay Maxted of the Survivors' Trust. The work of Women's Aid Ireland was also extremely useful.

Thank you to everyone at Audible and Amazon, especially Harriet Poland who was instrumental in shaping the book, Victoria Haslam, and Jack Ramm. Thanks also to Midas PR, and to Diana Beaumont and everyone at Marjacq, as always.

ABOUT THE AUTHOR

Photo © 2021 Donna Ford

Claire McGowan was born in 1981 in a small Irish village where the most exciting thing that ever happened was some cows getting loose on the road. She is the author of *The Fall*, *What You Did*, *The Other Wife*, *The Push*, *I Know You* and the acclaimed Paula Maguire crime series. She also writes women's fiction under the name Eva Woods.